500 Miles to Nowhere

The Legend of Bass Reeves

Fred Eason

Published by FastPencil

Copyright © 2012 Fred Eason

Published by FastPencil
3131 Bascom Ave.
Suite 150
Campbell CA 95008 USA
info@fastpencil.com
(408) 540-7571
(408) 540-7572 (Fax)
http://www.fastpencil.com

This work is fiction.

No part of this publication may be reproduced, stored in a retrieval system, or transmitted, in any form, or by any means, electronic, mechanical, photocopying, recording, or otherwise, without the prior consent of the publisher.

The Publisher makes no representations or warranties with respect to the accuracy or completeness of the contents of this book and specifically disclaim any implied warranties of merchantability or fitness for a particular purpose. Neither the publisher nor author shall be liable for any loss of profit or any commercial damages.

First Edition

I would like to dedicate this book to my father, Eben Obey Eason, who tried, without success, throughout his life to publish a novel.

Acknowledgements

This work was inspired by conversations with Bennie Westphal, who is a descendent of William P. Pittcock, depicted in this book, as well as the Westphal side of the family who were mainly railroad engineers. Bennie was most directly responsible for securing Fort Smith as the site for the new U. S. Marshal's Museum and first told me about Bass Reeves. I had never heard of Bass Reeves, but Bennie inspired me to research the subject through the several historical books that have been written about him, as stated in the introduction of this book.

I would also like to thank the team at FastPencil who helped to create this book: Mariena Foley was my project manager. Marian Jane Sanders edited this and my previous book and Matt O'Leary created two outstanding book covers for this and my previous book.

I would like to thank my son, Robert Eason, who also spent a lot of time editing and making suggestions to make the book more interesting.

Contents

	Foreword	ix
Chapter 1	He Needed Killing	1
Chapter 2	Homecoming and Leaving	19
Chapter 3	The Vendetta	35
Chapter 4	Billy's Plan Goes Wrong	53
Chapter 5	Parker Strikes Back	73
Chapter 6	Belle Starr	85
Chapter 7	Buffalo Bill Cody	105
Chapter 8	The Pursuit of Jesse James and Bob Dalton	117
Chapter 9	The Upbringing	137
Chapter 10	The Trial of Billy Washington and Dick McLish	157
Chapter 11	Another Train Robbery	179
Chapter 12	The Trial of Bass Reeves and Robert's Marriage	193
Chapter 13	A Dastardly Crime	209
Chapter 14	The Shootout	219

Foreword

This book is based on some true stories about Bass Reeves and some fictional stories about Bass Reeves imagined by the author. By all historical accounts, Bass was an exceptional U.S. Marshal serving under Judge Parker's Court. According to history, he was selected by Judge Parker because of his previous experience as a bounty hunter out of the prior Van Buren Court. He was also selected because of his ability to speak all of the Indian languages. He learned their languages while he was a runaway slave during and after the Civil War. His race did not seem to be an issue with Judge Parker, although it was obvious that there was a lot of prejudice during that time among white people. The most interesting thing about Bass Reeves, as only one of a handful of black marshals, is that the vast majority of criminals in the Indian Territory were white. One could imagine the potential conflicts involving a black lawman and mostly white criminals.
During his lifetime, Bass became friends with Belle Star, who was friends with Frank James and Bob Dalton and other interesting characters of the time. Many of the

events in this book are fictional, even though many of the characters were real. History does not say that Colonel George Reeves was the father of Bass Reeves. The author simply draws that conclusion in the book based upon the relationship between the two men and the fact that both Bass and his mother lived in the Reeves' home and were treated like family.

The time period covered is the time when Judge Parker's court was the only law that existed other than the Indian Police, the "Lighthorse." Criminals were executed by order of Parker, with no appeal to a higher court. That period covers the time from 1875, when Judge Parker began to preside, until the court was ended in 1896. Even though he caused many men to be put to death, history shows that Judge Parker was against capital punishment. The geography of the events in the book are historically correct, occurring in the Indian Territory which is now the State of Oklahoma.

Deputy U.S. Marshals, J.H. Mershon, William P. Pittcock, Bud Kell and Heck Thomas were all living and working for U.S. Marshal Colonel Thomas Boles and Judge Parker at that time.

This book is primarily fiction which is loosely based upon the life of Bass Reeves, and is not intended to be historically correct.

There are a number of very good books which discuss the actual history of Bass Reeves. Perhaps the most historically correct book was *Black Gun, Silver Star*, written by Art T. Burton. Art T. Burton was a professor of history at South Suburban College in South Holland, Illinois. He also wrote the book *Black, Buckskin, and Blue* and the book, *Black, Red, and Deadly.*

Paul L. Brady wrote a book *The Black Badge* that includes interviews with descendants of Bass Reeves, which would include Paul L. Brady. In 1972, Brady was the first African American to be appointed as a Federal Administrative Law Judge, where he served for 25 years.

There is also a book that was written for children by R. Gregory Christie called *Bad News for Outlaws, The Remarkable Life of Bass Reeves, Deputy U.S. Marshal.*

The "Bible" for facts regarding Judge Isaac C. Parker's court, is called *Hell on the Border*, written in about 1898 by S.W. Harman and C.P. Sterns. Many of the facts in this novel were taken from this great book. Parts of Judge Parker's famous charge to a Grand Jury has been used from the above source.

Wikipedia also provided some interesting facts about the life of Bass Reeves.

All of the above books can be ordered from Amazon.com.

1

He Needed Killing

Jim Webb jumped out of a window of Bywaters' store and made a run for his horse, but deputy U.S. Marshal Bass Reeves rode up on his horse and ordered the outlaw to surrender. Bass had been trying to catch the outlaw for two years and he wasn't about to let him get away. The outlaw turned and started shooting at the marshal with his rifle, grazing the marshal's saddle horn with his first shot and shattering a button on his coat with the second and then blasting the reins right out of the marshal's hands with the third shot. With the sounds of BOOM! BOOM! BOOM! still ringing in his ears and the turbulence of the bullets narrowly missing his body, the marshal dove off his horse, landed on his feet and aimed his own Winchester rifle at the outlaw and fired twice, with both rounds hitting the man and ending the fight, but not before a fourth .44 caliber bullet from the outlaw's rifle had put a hole in the brim of the marshal's hat. He was still a bit rattled by the close misses as he walked over to the outlaw.

As Bass approached the outlaw, he had just enough life left to utter "I have killed eleven men and expected for you to be the twelfth. Take my guns as your prize. You earned them." The marshal took Webb's pistol and put it in his saddle bag and attached Webb's rifle to his saddle. He then tied Webb's body to his horse to carry him back to the prison wagon. He took the man's saddle to the livery stable and sold it to pay for Webb's burial. The marshal saved Webb's boots and gun belt to show to Judge Parker so he could collect his reward.

Jim Webb had a $5,000 bounty on his head, as he had "skipped out" on a $17,000 bond and the marshal would be happy to collect it. $5,000 was a lot of money in 1884. This reward would be used to invest in more top notch horses on the farm he owned in Van Buren, just across the river from Fort Smith, where Judge Parker's court was held. He would have preferred not to have killed Webb, but had no choice in the matter. His orders as a U.S. Marshal, serving under Judge Parker were to bring them in dead or alive. Reeves was angry about Webb getting out of jail on bond after he had arrested him in the first place.

The marshal rode a beautiful sorrel, a reddish-brown horse, with a light colored mane. Most marshals owned fine horses that were capable of catching ordinary horses. Sometimes outlaws would be tipped off about who a marshal was by the way they sat in the saddle and by the quality of their horses and saddles. There were only 3 other negro marshals, besides Bass, at that time and someone had seen the marshal coming and tipped Webb off.

Successful marshals made a lot of money and spared no expense when it came to fine horses or guns. This marshal tended to wear a bow-tie and suit, even on a dusty trail. He wore a pair of Colt 1873 Single Action Army .45 revolvers, carried in a black handmade "cross-draw" leather holster rig with the backs of the handles facing to the front. Most who saw that rig knew who he was. He also carried a Winchester .38-.40 carbine in a scabbard attached to his saddle. He pondered a moment on why he had gone for the rifle in his scabbard instead of the Colts. He guessed it was just instinctive due to the other man having a rifle. Usually he preferred the Colts at close range. He was ambidextrous and could draw either or both Colts just as well and shoot them equally well. He was just as good with his rifle with either hand. No matter which direction an outlaw came from, he could react quickly. He was 46-years-old at the time, but could still hold his own in a fist fight. At 6-feet, two-inches and 200 pounds, he was still in good shape for his age. He was an impressive figure, taller than most men of his time. He was a man who did not think very much about himself. He did not feel like being colored was an advantage or a disadvantage. He figured his abilities spoke more about him as a man than did his color. And most men of any color respected him for that.

All U.S. Marshals at that time were required to travel with a chuck wagon and cook, a "prison" wagon and guard, and one hired gun or posse man. It was not unusual to accumulate 10 to 15 outlaws on a single trip and someone had to guard them and feed them while the marshal was hunting down other outlaws that might be in the area. Sometimes he took the posse man with him to make an arrest and sometimes he went by himself.

The marshal was on his way back to the wagon, which already held ten prisoners, when he came across an angry mob in the process of lynching a man who had been accused of stealing cattle. The ranch hands had tracked him down and were about to administer their own form of justice. The marshal rode into the crowd and proclaimed, "I'm Bass Reeves, United States Marshal, and I'll take this man to Judge Parker's court. You can come to Fort Smith and have charges filed against him and he'll get a fair trial."

"Like Hell you will!" one of the ranch hands screamed. "We caught him and we aim to hang him right here."

One of the other ranch hands restrained the man and said, "You don't want to mess with this marshal. As you can see, he's already killed Jim Webb who's tied to the horse behind him. He can kill you or whip you either way you want."

"I'd like to see him whip my ass!" the ranch hand countered, seemingly not intimidated by the dead man.

Bass calmly stepped down off his horse and said "You can have the first punch." The ranch hand stepped down from his horse and threw a punch and Bass countered with a punch that knocked the man to the ground. He didn't get up. The marshal thought for a moment he'd have to draw his Colts and had his hands in the position to do so, but the crowd seemed to calm down when they saw he was willing to draw. Most of them knew he was fast as lightning and they'd just witnessed him knocking down the biggest cowboy they had with them. They knew the man he'd killed, Jim Webb, had been a foreman on their ranch. Bass had a reputation and they knew he wasn't going to back down, so they did. Bass cut the man they were going to lynch down and took him to his wagon, along with Jim Webb. He tied the man to the horse behind Webb. He figured the horse could carry two people, no further than they were going.

The next day, the marshal and his cook and wagons all headed back to Fort Smith. It had been a very profitable trip. He had close to $900 in fees due to him, besides the bounty on Webb. Even after paying the cook $20 per month, a guard $3 per day and a posse man $3 per day and paying for all their food and other expenses, he had a nice deposit for the bank. His herd of fine horses was growing and he'd be able to retire in comfort whenever he got tired of the trail. Most of his horses were top of the line and would bring $100 each or more. He was living a good life, although dangerous, but the journey to this point had not been easy.

They were more than 80 miles west of Fort Smith, past the zone known as the "dead line." The dead line was where outlaws posted threats to any lawman who might be looking for them saying if they crossed this line they'd soon be dead. As they passed through the area, on the way back to Fort Smith, Bass was amused to find a note from Jim Webb that said, "Bass Reeves, if you cross this line and attempt to arrest me, you'll soon be dead." He pulled the note from the tree and added it to his collection. Bass had crossed this line many times and had been shot at many times, but had been wounded only one time. The dead line ran north and south through Fort Gibson and Muskogee, and followed the North to South path of the Missouri, Kansas and Texas Rail Road.

The only law in the Indian Territory, besides U. S. Marshals who traveled there, were Indian police, known as "Lighthorse". The Lighthorse only had jurisdiction over Indians or Indian freedmen. Indian freedmen were negro slaves who'd been traded for or bought by Indians and freed after the Civil War. The marshal's territory covered the Indian Nation, where Indians had been herded to from all over the country across the Trail of Tears.

The Indians had been given these lands under a treaty that had since been challenged, due to the Indian Nation's perceived support of the Confederacy. There were roughly 25,000 white men living in the Indian territory and at least 20,000 of them were outlaws preying on the Indians or the railroads or the ranchers. The fact they were white didn't stop Bass from arresting or killing them. Justice, in Judge Parker's Court, was indifferent to race.

Many of the arrests that Bass made were for "introducing," which was the illegal practice of selling whiskey or other alcoholic beverages to the Indians. But there were also many thieves, murderers and rapists that he dealt with.

Some of the outlaws made a good living robbing the Atchison, Topeka & Santa Fe Rail Road, the Rock Island, Pacific Rail Road,the Kansas and Arkansas Valley Rail Road, the Missouri, Kansas & Texas Rail Road or the St. Louis & San Francisco Rail Road. Most of the best rewards were paid by the railroads.

The Indian Territory consisted of the Cherokee, Osage, Cheyenne, Arapaho, Wichita, Caddo, Comanche, Kiowa, Apache, Chickasaw, Creek and Choctaw Indians. Bass had lived with the Indians for many years as a runaway slave and knew almost all of the Indian leaders and their policemen and spoke most of the Indian languages fluently. That gave him an edge over the other marshals. The Lighthorse and other Indians he knew fed him information regarding a certain outlaw's whereabouts.

After the first day of travel, the group stopped to camp for the night and the prisoners were all attached to a long, heavy chain outside the wagon. That way they could be fed and could sleep more comfortably overnight. The negro cook, William Leach, was busy cooking the nightly meal, complete with biscuits and a big pot of stew, over an open fire. He had already cooked the meat for the stew in a big frying pan. Bass went over and got himself a biscuit to chew on prior to the meal. His dog, Bandit, was standing on his hind legs and begging for a share. Bass threw the dog a couple of bites, which really made the cook mad and he told Bass so. The cook had a really bad temper and that had bothered Bass in the past. He had also been in trouble before and Judge Parker had thrown him in jail a few times, but he was a good cook.

Bass ignored the cook and began to clean his rifle. He had shot some game with it for the cook and wanted to clean it before he needed it again. He was unloading the rifle, one shell at a time, when he realized a cartridge that was in the chamber seemed to be stuck. When he looked at it, he realized that the cartridge must have had a dent in it and the rifle would not eject it. He was trying to pry the cartridge from the chamber with his pocket knife. About this time he glanced up to see Bandit standing up begging the cook to give him a piece of leftover stew meat from the big frying pan he had in his hand. Bass loved Bandit like he loved all of his animals. Instead of giving the dog a piece of meat, the cook threw the whole pan of scalding grease on the dog and down his mouth. The dog took his last breath and died. Bass jumped to his feet and his rifle went off, shooting the stuck round, killing the cook on the spot. The posseman and the prisoners weren't sure if his sudden reaction caused the gun to go off, or if Bass was defending his dog. The grief welled up inside Bass. He wanted to cry but would not let himself cry in front of all of these men.

There were too many witnesses to deny what had happened. Judge Parker was not very forgiving of a lawman who broke the law. He did not know what he was going to do. Killing a man over a dog would probably not sit well with Judge Parker, even though it might have been an accident.

It would be a long night and a long next day without food, so he ordered his posse man to cook something from the wagon. Meanwhile, he continued to prise the spent .38-.40 round out of the chamber of the rifle and finish cleaning the rifle so that it would be ready the next day.

The next morning, after they had packed the wagons and the prisoners, along with the dead cook, the marshal and his men resumed the trip back to Fort Smith. He started to think about the first man he had killed on this trip, Jim Webb. Webb was an outlaw who had drifted into the Chickasaw Nation from Texas and had gone to work for Billy Washington, a prominent rancher who was a partner with Dick McLish, a prominent Chickasaw Indian. They owned a huge ranch in the southern portion of the Chickasaw Nation and were very wealthy. Webb became the foreman of the ranch and supervised 45 cowboys and 7 gun hands, several of whom were negros and Indians. Webb ran the ranch with an iron hand, and nobody contested that.

A negro preacher, William Steward, owned a small ranch that joined the Washington-McLish Ranch. He had set a fire on his ranch that spread out of control to the bigger ranch next door. Jim Webb was furious about it and rode over to the preacher's ranch to confront him. After a violent argument, Webb drew his gun and killed the preacher. After Bass had been given a warrant for Webb's arrest, he went to the ranch to serve the warrant, along with Floyd Wilson, a posseman. When they arrived at the ranch, there were only a few men there. They did not have on their badges and stopped to ask if they could share some breakfast. Webb was immediately suspicious of the men. He kept his hand on his gun the whole time that Bass and Floyd were eating. Eventually, out on the porch with Webb and another gunman who worked at the ranch, Webb took his eye off the marshal just long enough for Bass to put his arm around Webb's neck and draw his gun. The marshal aimed it at the other gunman, who still reached for his gun and shot at Bass. Bass returned fire and shot him right between his eyes. After his arrest, Webb had skipped bail and was on the run until Bass caught up with him again.

As they continued their journey to Fort Smith, gunshots rang out and bullets starting pelting the ground around the marshal and his group. There were 6 gunmen on a nearby hill, shooting at them with rifles. They were about 300 yards away. The marshal drew his rifle and killed three of the men. He then rode his horse straight at the men while continuing to fire his rifle. By the time he reached the top of the hill, the remaining 3 men had managed to reach their horses and were heading towards Muskogee, which was towards the Washington-McLish Ranch.

Bass had been heading east from the Chickasaw Nation.

He guessed that the ranch hands who had been trying to hang the man who was now his prisoner had told the owners of the ranch about that. When they told the owners about him killing Webb, they had probably sent the gun hands to try to kill him. He managed to kill two more of the men, while chasing them. They were surprised by how fast he had overtaken them and had been looking back at him with fear in their eyes. They knew they were dead men. They were riding $20 horses while he was riding a sorrel which probably would have fetched $150, even at that time.

He let the last man ride off, because he wanted the man to go back to the ranch and tell the owners. Maybe they would think twice before sending anyone after him again. Judge Parker always said it was the fear of certain punishment that caused a man to do right. Bass wanted them to feel that fear. It was to his advantage, or so he thought at the time.

The marshal collected the men's horses and tied their bodies to them in order to take them back to his waiting chuck and prison wagon. The guard and posse man had been of little help to him. Even though they had rifles, they probably could not have made the shots that Bass had made. That's why he made the kind of money he made. Most men would not have attempted to do the things he did to make a living. Out of a total of about 200 deputy U.S. Marshals who had worked for Judge Parker's court in Fort Smith, over the years, almost half had been killed. One died in an insane asylum and some just quit and some were severely wounded. Very few had lasted as many years as Bass. Every time he left Fort Smith in search of prisoners he realized he might not return alive, but he could not help but love the job. The marshal knew he was helping the Indians who had been so good to him when he was a runaway.

As the group rode into Fort Smith, they gathered immediate attention and a crowd started to follow. Scenes like this were the main entertainment in Fort Smith. This was the show that proceeded the big show: the hangings. The marshal rode tall and proud in his saddle, like the returning warrior that he was. Most of the people in town admired him. All feared him. Some hated him.

Once they arrived at the jail, the task began of unloading the prisoners, who were shackled to a long chain and led into the jail building. The guard and the posse man helped Bass lock them up for transport, being careful not to give any of them the chance to reach a gun. The transfer went without incident for a change. It was not unusual for one or more of the prisoners to attempt an escape at this point in the trip.

After Bass unloaded his prisoners and took care of the burial of the dead outlaws and Jim Webb, the marshal went in to see Judge Parker. Normally he loved going to see the judge. The judge cared about Bass as if he were a son and spent many hours teaching him the law. Most of the marshals that worked for the judge were close to being outlaws themselves and he had a hard time keeping them from doing wrong. Judge Parker had been forced to charge several of his deputies with murder over the years, just for killing people with no good reason. In fact, he required each marshal to write him and ask for a writ before they were allowed to arrest a person that did not have a writ against them from the judge to begin with. The exception would be where they witnessed a crime as it happened. Sometimes, if they were Indians, the Lighthorse would already have them under arrest and a marshal simply took custody from them.

"Good job, marshall," Judge Parker said, "I see you have brought in 10 live men and I heard you had to kill Jim Webb?"

"Yes sir," Bass replied to the judge "and I had to kill 5 gunmen who I think were sent from the Washington-McLish Ranch to avenge Webb's death. They ambushed us on the way back to Fort Smith. I let one of them escape, so he could tell them what happened. Maybe that will stop them from trying that again."

"I doubt that will stop those people." Parker replied. "They don't seem to have any sense in spite of being wealthy. Well, I think the court owes you about $5,900. There was a $5,000 bounty on Webb put up by the bonding agent when Webb skipped out on a $17,000 bail and we owe you another $900 in fees according to your report on distance and arrests. Are you going to buy more horses with the money?"

"Yes sir," Bass answered. "And I also hate to tell you this, but I killed my negro cook."

"How did that happen?," the judge replied.

"Well sir, I was cleaning my rifle when the cook threw a frying pan full of hot grease on my dog Bandit when I just jumped up and my rifle went off. I know that wasn't the right thing to happen. I rescued that dog from a cruel owner and just got him to trust me. I don't know what else to say. I guess I should have been more careful with the rifle. I'm sorry."

The judge was thinking about what Bass had just told him. He knew the big man loved his animals like they were his own children and he was the best deputy he had, so he hated to lose him. But he was a judge sworn to uphold the law.

"Bass, you know that you may have broken the law. I am not going to have you arrested and I want you to continue to do your job, but you will have to stand trial. I may call a Grand Jury hearing to determine if you should be charged. I am very busy dealing with much worse criminals right now, so what I am going to do is to set you up with a trial date about 2 years from now. As your friend, I would advise you to hire one of the very best attorneys in Fort Smith and you know who they are. If it were me, I would hire someone from the law firm of William H.H. Clayton, William M. Cravens and Thomas Marcum. Clayton, as you know, is the District Attorney."

"I don't have to worry about you not showing up for trial," the judge continued, "with a wife and kids and property nearby, so there will be no warrants or any bail. But you will have to stand for a trial or Grand Jury hearing. It's possible that when you jumped up while extracting the shells from your rifle, like you said, you could have killed the cook accidentally. But your lawyer will have to deal with that and we will probably have to have a jury, since I would probably not be able to render an unbiased opinion when it comes to you. The prisoners you had with you would probably not make good witnesses in court, but your posse man and guard might have to testify. Understand?"

"Yessir," Bass replied.

He was somewhat relieved, because the judge didn't seem to be mad at him. The judge had dealings with the cook before and had put him in jail a few times for cheating at cards and being drunk and for shooting another man's dog and for beating a horse. As far as Judge Parker was concerned, the man needed killing, but the public would probably not tolerate him letting Bass off without a trial. He knew that President Grant would probably pardon Bass, at his request, if he happened to get convicted. He was far more concerned with cleaning up the Indian Territory, which covered 74,000 square miles.

Bass was more concerned with going home to his ranch and seeing his wife and kids and extended family. He had bought the ranch with money he had earned as a bounty hunter out of the Van Buren court before Judge Parker's court existed.

Once Bass had determined he was going to settle down, he went to Fort Gibson to ask Jennie to marry him. She was part white, part Indian and part negro. He had met her when he was living among the Indians during the Civil War. It was then that he had learned to speak Muskogee, the language of the Creeks and Seminoles and had learned to speak the languages of the all the tribes that inhabited the Indian Territory. Many slaves had escaped into the Indian Territory during the Civil War and were accepted by the Indians, even though some Indians had traded for and owned negro slaves of their own. After the

Civil War, the slaves became "Indian Freedmen". As a part of the 1866 treaty, those freedmen became members of the Indian tribes. Many negros married or otherwise integrated with the Indians.

Bass had built 3 houses on the ranch. One for he and Jennie and their children and one for his mother Pearlalee and one for his sister, Jane and her husband. Jane's husband ran the ranch while Bass was out rounding up outlaws. He viewed his family as his most valued asset. The ranch and horses came next. He had bought a beautiful property on a plateau overlooking the Arkansas River and Fort Smith, on top of Mount Vista. He could stand on the edge of his property and see the river winding around Fort Smith and heading West into the Indian Territory and he could look downriver to where the river separated Van Buren and Fort Smith. When bad weather approached, it usually came from the Southwest and he could see it coming from miles away. That allowed them to make sure the livestock and the family were safely inside. Tornadoes usually seemed to follow the river, but as far as he knew, none had ever jumped up onto the plateau, although the wind could be pretty dangerous. There were some people who thought he was "uppity" and he guessed he was pretty "uppity", setting up on his mountain. Looking down at all of the land below him did make him feel pretty special. Once he had managed to buy all of the land on the plateau, he started expanding his land on the flatlands below the mountain.

He had purchased most of the land for about $5 per acre. Most of his best pasture land was on the flatlands below the mountain. He had bought the land on the plateau for $2 per acre. One of the reasons that Bass had selected the plateau as the place to build his home, other than the vast beauty of it, was he felt like his family was safe there. There was only one trail up the mountain and one or two armed men could hold off an army of men trying to come up the trail. He had made a lot of enemies and a lot of dangerous men would like to see him dead. He was worried that some of those men might get the idea of harming or capturing his family to get to him. It gave him great comfort when he was 250 miles or more West of Fort Smith to know that his family was safe on the mountain. His brother-in-law, Green Saunders, was a good rancher and was a good shot with a rifle and made it a point to keep an eye on the trail.

He had several ranch hands, who were Indian, who also helped to keep an eye on the trail. Someone was watching it 24 hours a day. There was also a giant bolder at the top of the trail that could be set to roll down the mountain with a charge of dynamite if that became necessary. He hoped they never had to resort to that, since it would be a lot of work to clean up the trail again. It had taken them almost a year to build the trail, one stick of dynamite and one wagon load of rock at a time. Most of the folks in Van Buren thought Bass was crazy to buy a piece of property like that and even crazier to build a house up there. It was a lot of extra work to get all the building materials to the top of the hill, although they cut most of the lumber off the top of the plateau.

Bass was not afraid of hard work and knew that being a marshal was dangerous. So he had to plan for that and be prepared for the worst. He could rest at ease with his family living in the "fortress" he had built for them on the hill.

2

Homecoming and Leaving

By the time Bass got to the top of Mount Vista, he had to remind himself of why he had built on top of this hill. The trail up there was really giving his horse a workout. But he figured any horse that could make it up this hill could probably catch any horse around. There was one horse at the ranch that could outrun the sorrel, known to him as "Rusty". He wasn't sure of the lineage, but the horse was solid white. He called the horse "Silver", because sometimes the sun reflecting off the horse seemed to reflect some hair that looked just like it was made of silver. Besides, "Whitey" just didn't seem right. He loved to ride Silver, but was saving the stallion for a special trip. He did not want everyone to know he had a white horse. Right now, everyone expected to see him on a sorrel. He actually had several sorrels that he rode on different occasions. He always wanted to have a horse that was as rested and well fed as possible. Fast horses gave him the same advantage that his ability with firearms did. Having an edge of any kind might make the difference between staying alive or being dead.

As Bass rode up to the house, his wife Jennie and his eight children, Sarah, the oldest, Robert, the second oldest, Harriet, the third oldest and Georgia, Alice, Newland, Edgar and Lula, in the order of birth, all came running up to him while the youngest kids screamed, "Daddy, daddy, daddy!" As soon as he got down off Rusty, they all hugged his neck one at a time. This is what I'm working for, he thought, as he hugged them back. This is what the marshal looked forward to the whole time he was gone. This is what kept him motivated while he was out risking his life and dealing with scumbags and killers. He then gave Jennie a big kiss and they headed into the house.

Bass had built the house from oak logs he cut off the plateau. It was a simple structure that had a kitchen and large sitting area on one side of a "breeze-way" and the parents' bedroom and five bunkrooms for the kids on the other. The breeze-way served as a middle sitting area and connected to a porch facing west that looked down on Fort Smith. The wind, which usually came from the west or south during the summer, was forced between the two halves of the house that served to funnel the wind through the breeze-way. It was pretty cool on the porch even on a typical summer day in Arkansas. All of the bedrooms and the living area had windows that let a lot of air blow throughout the house. The breeze-way also siphoned the air through the other parts of the house. Bass loved to sit on the porch in the afternoon and watch the sun setting over the Indian Territory to the west. He imagined he could see all the way to the dead line.

When it came time for supper, Jennie told him that she had invited his mother and sister and her husband to eat with them. Bass had bought a giant bison roast in Fort Smith and she had been cooking it for hours, along with fresh vegetables from her garden, including black-eyed peas, cabbage and fresh sliced tomatoes. She had baked a big slab of the bison in a big metal pot along with fresh potatoes and carrots and onions. Bass was drooling at the prospect of such a meal. While they were on the trail, they pretty much ate whatever they could kill. Bass and his family were extremely religious and they always said prayers for the meal and his safe return before every meal, whether he was there or not. If he was there, they would thank God for his safe return. In the sitting area of the kitchen, they had several large tables with chairs to seat all 13 of them when they scooted all of the tables together.

While they were eating, Bass decided to conduct some business and told his brother-in-law, Green Saunders, that he had brought back enough money to add some more fine horses to their stables.

"Green," Bass began, "after adding to our savings account, I think we have enough extra money to add another 10 really good horses to the herd. You may want to check and see where we could get some really good ones. I'd be willing to pay $100 each for the best ones you can find."

"I'll check around and see where I can find what you're looking for. Maybe we can buy some thoroughbred stock out of Texas. I've seen some real nice herds brought through Fort Smith on their way to different places, but wasn't sure if we were going to buy or sell at this point," Green replied.

"I trust your judgement," Bass continued. "Just remember, I might be running for my life on one of these horses, so only buy horses you'd trust with your life."

"I understand." Green said.

Green started to think about where he might go to find some really good horses. Even the army was not as picky about horses as Bass was. Every one in Arkansas knew the herd they were raising included the finest horses available. Most of the other marshals bought their horses from Bass. They didn't want to be outran either. Most were willing to pay up to $150 for one of his horses and several had tried to buy horses that Bass kept for himself, but were told they were not for sale.

After supper, Jennie gave Bass a pipe she had bought for him in Fort Smith, along with some fancy imported tobacco. It was one of those pipes that was shaped kind of like an "S", with the burning part dropping below his chin. He thought he looked like a detective when he smoked it. Jennie thought it made him look distinguished. He enjoyed sitting on the porch and smoking it while Jennie and the girls finished cleaning up the table. Jennie had also bought him a nice oversized rocking chair that was considered to be his that no other person sat in. He was a big man and was thankful for the big rocking chair.

All of the children had their own chores to do. Sallie, who was 21 and the oldest, was now more than old enough to be married and needed to learn all of her mother's cooking skills. Bass's sister Jane, who did all of the sewing on the ranch, including all of his clothing, was also teaching Sallie to sew.

His oldest son, Robert, now 19 and Newland, now 12, worked for Green, taking care of the horses. The best horses were still kept at the stables on Mount Vista. These stables were some of the nicest and cleanest stables you would find anywhere. The horses that Bass kept for his own personal use were kept in stables all by themselves. Each had a separate stall where they were groomed and shoed.

Green was teaching the oldest boys what to feed the horses and how to keep them well groomed. He was teaching Robert how to be a blacksmith, which was a skill he and Bass both shared. Robert was old enough to go out on his own or become a marshal himself, but so far had been happy to stay on the family farm and Bass was happy to have him there. He loved all of his kids and hated to see the moment when they might leave.

He thought Sallie would be married and gone by now, but was happy to have her stay. She was a big help to Jennie and helped take care of Pearlalee, his mother, who was getting to be about 65 years old by now. In fact, Sallie had moved into the house that Bass had built for Pearlalee so that she could see after her more closely. There was enough work on the ranch for everyone and all of the kids did their fair share.

While Jennie was finishing up in the kitchen, Bass decided to walk Sallie and Pearlalee back to their house. He had something on his mind he wanted to ask his mother and wanted to get her alone. She was getting old so he wanted to get as much family history from her as he could. She was pretty good about sitting with the children and telling them stories about Bass as a child. According to her, his father was a freedman who crossed her path while she was a servant for the Reeves family in Texas. However, he had heard otherwise and intended to confront her before she got too old to remember. After asking Sallie to give them some privacy, Bass asked his mother, "Who did you say my father was?"

"I've told you who your father was," she responded, slightly angry at her son's tone.

"Well, as you know, I spent a lot of time growing up with our master, Colonel George Reeves and even went with him into the Civil War when he fought for the Confederacy where I learned to shoot and ride well enough to survive myself and to help protect him. We got to be very close and I considered him to be my friend. One night, we were drinking in a bar and playing cards when he called me son. I looked him straight in the eye and said 'you're not my father, why're you calling me son?' He said, 'you are my son'. I was so mad that I jumped up and hit him and that's when I ran off to the Indian Territory. Nobody ever came looking for me. He never put a bounty on me like most other runaway slaves. Why would he say something like that?"

Pearlalee looked at him with tears in her eyes and said "I hoped you would never find out. You know we lived in his house and I loved his wife and didn't want to do what he wanted to do, but couldn't do anything about it. That's why he showed you off like he did. He was really proud of you, but I didn't think he'd ever admit to bein' your father. That's why he taught you to be a blacksmith and why he taught you to take care of his horses. You know his wife couldn't bear him any children and the longer he was around you the more he came to realize you were his. He bragged to me about you all of the time. He was going to leave all his horses to you."

"I didn't want any of his damn horses!" Bass responded angrily, "I have my own horses! I can't believe he did that to you. It makes me want to go find him and kill him."

"Son," Pearlalee said, looking him in the eye, "God doesn't want you to feel that way about your father, even if he became your father against my will.

Your father was a great man, in spite of what he did to me. He was Speaker of the House of Representatives for the State of Texas and Reeves County in Texas was named for him. You shouldn't hate him. His greatness is in you. Even when you were a child, everyone knew you weren't an ordinary child. I love the greatness in you that he gave you. For that reason, I forgave him for what he did to me.

He wanted children of his own and he got you. If you ever do see him again, you should learn to love him like your children love you, even though you are a much better father than he was. He taught you how to shoot and ride horses. You make a good living doing that. I never loved him but he loved you and loved the part of you that was him. Can't you forgive him like I did?"

"Maybe," Reeves said. He knew his mother was right. "What about Jane? Who's her father?"

"Jane's your half sister. Her father is the man that I said was your father. I'm sorry I lied to you about this. I just though it would be best. You know that us slaves were not allowed to get married."

"I never thought I would be 46-years-old when I found out who my real father was," Bass continued, "but it does make a lot of sense to me now that I know. I have been thinking about this ever since the colonel and I got into a fight at that card game. I wanted to ask you that question all of these years and I just couldn't let you die with me not knowing the truth. I don't plan to try to contact him. I have my own family to think of now. I don't plan to tell anyone else about this."

"That's probably for the best," Pearlalee responded, "There's no reason to upset the rest of the family."

"Jennie has white blood, Indian blood and negro blood in her, so I'm sure she would understand me being mixed," Bass continued, "but I don't plan to bring this up unless she does."

"I won't either," Pearlalee said, "and I'm really sorry I didn't tell you this sooner."

"That's not a problem mama," Bass allowed, "I suspected it for a long time."

The walk back to the main house seemed further to Bass as he pondered the conversation he had just had with his mother. He was way past worrying about what his heritage was. He now had to worry about the legacy he would leave. He just had to know the truth…..now he did. That was the end of it as far as he was concerned.

When he got back to the main house, Jennie had finished cleaning up and had just taken a bath. She was sitting in a rocker on the porch in a bathrobe. Her fresh scrubbed skin was glowing in the sunset. Her hair was straight, like the Indian in her, and her eyes were a beautiful shade of hazel. He'd thought about what beautiful eyes she had from the moment he met her in Indian territory. She'd always loved his brown eyes that had a touch of green in them. But what she really loved about him was the proud way he carried himself, like a great stallion. There was no uncertainty about him. He had confidence in himself. Even at 46, after chasing outlaws on horses for years, he still stood erect and proud. The kids were in bed and this was their special time together. There were some clouds in the sky and the sun was painting them in beautiful shades of red and gold. He looked at her and felt really lucky to be home with her again.

Jennie had been educated in the mission schools in Indian Territory, while living in the Creek Nation and later working with Chief Opothle Yahola, chief of the

Upper Creeks. She was gradually teaching Bass to read and write. He could already do numbers in his head. The ranch financials and their savings were all kept in his head.

The next morning Bass was greeted with biscuits and gravy along with fresh eggs and ham. Everything that they needed was produced on the ranch. In addition to the horses, they had chickens, turkeys, geese, goats, pigs and one mule. They used the mule to plow the garden. They owned pastureland in the valley below that produced good grazing and an ample supply of hay for the winter. They managed to raise enough corn to feed the children and all of the other livestock. The horses that Bass rode got corn and oats when they had them. The only thing missing was a dog. Bass missed Bandit and vowed to find another dog soon. Bandit would always wake him up if anything was wrong.

After breakfast, Bass made his tour of the farm on Rusty, riding alongside Green on another sorrel. He inspected the barns and stalls like a general barking out instructions about what could be done better to Green, who passed those instructions down to the kids. They were always happy to see him come home, but were somewhat relieved when he left. He kept them all running when he was there and expected perfection.

As they passed Green's house, Bass's sister Jane came out to greet him and let him know that she had a brand new suit of clothes for him to wear on his next trip. Some would say that it was silly for a lawman to wear a suit while in pursuit. Many times, he would have to cross waterways and sometimes crawl on his hands and knees to capture criminals, but he would not budge on the clothing. It made him feel special when he put on a suit that he knew took Jane weeks to finish. It made Jane feel special to have a brother that took pride in wearing what she made. It also made her proud that Bass trusted her husband with his prized livestock and with running his business and picking out the animals. Bass was gone for weeks at a time chasing bad guys, so he was happy to have someone like Green to take care of everything when he was gone.

After his tour, he sat down with Green to discuss the business. "It seems to me that we're going to have to add to the stables," Bass said matter-of-factly, "when we add those 10 horses to the herd. And we may have to move more horses down the hill to our other pastures. I've saved enough money to buy some more land if it comes down to that, but I think we'll be O.K. for the time being."

"I think we need to start checking around to see if we can buy some more land," Green said, "we may not be able to find land for sale when we need it. We should probably add more land than we need when we have a chance. I heard about another 100 acres of pasture that might be for sale in a month or two that touches our property in the valley. The man who owned it died and his children are going to auction it off. They don't live here any more and don't care anything about the land or the house. We could either tear the house down, or use it to store hay. The metal roof looks like it is in good shape. We might have to tear a few walls down to make more room, but I don't think they are load bearing. If they are, we can put up some poles for support."

"All right," Bass answered, "why don't you keep an eye on that and go ahead and bid on it when the time comes. We can probably buy it for $5 an acre, but I'd go as high as $10 per acre, since it has a house on it. I plan on continuing to buy horses when I can and sell as few as I need to, as long as we make a good profit on them."

"Speaking of that," Green said, "the army wanted to buy 10 horses from us, for their officers to ride, but they only wanted to pay about $50 per horse for them. I didn't think that'd be enough and told them so."

"We don't have any horses I'd sell for that," Bass allowed, "they'll either have to come up in price or look for horses somewhere else."

"That's what I thought you'd say," Green replied. "They're still thinking about it. One of the officers really wanted Silver, but I told him Silver was not for sale for any price. He was willing to pay $50 more out of his pocket to buy that horse."

"You were right," Bass said, "he didn't have enough money to buy Silver. He's mine to ride and he'll produce some really fine colts that we can get good money for. That makes him worth a lot of money to me."

Bass really enjoyed being home for about a week. Then, something inside him that he could not explain, began to make him restless. He guessed he had become addicted to the excitement of being on the hunt. He enjoyed hunting outlaws as much as some men liked hunting rabbits.

After being home for about a week, he decided it was time to ride back to Fort Smith and see what Judge Parker had for him to do. Jennie always hated to see him pack up and leave, but she knew that was the way he was when they married, and knew that's how he made a living. Jennie worried that he'd be hurt or killed. He worried about that a little himself. He couldn't imagine making a living any other way and he never thought much about retiring, even though he knew that he probably had enough money saved and enough income from selling horses to support a good retirement.

There were tearful goodbyes as he left the ranch and headed to the courthouse in Fort Smith. He'd decided to give Rusty some time off and had Green saddle another one of his sorrels that he called "Midnight." Midnight was such a dark brown that he was almost black. He had a white patch on his forehead that was shaped like a diamond. Midnight was not as fast as Silver but was a little faster than Rusty.

On his way to meet U. S. Marshal Colonel Thomas Boles, Bass thought back to the terrible smell that used to rise up into the courthouse and marshal's office from the old jail cells below. The old jail in Fort Smith had long been known as "Hell on the Border". It had been located under the courtroom and marshal's office and was two large rooms about 29 feet by 55 feet each. The prisoners were allowed to mingle with each other in these two large spaces. The jail resembled a dungeon. It could hold up to 150 prisoners. There were white men and negroes and Indians all mingled together. Bedding was moldy and the place had smelled like urine and feces. Hell on the Border was a good name for it. Thankfully it was now empty and cleaner.

In 1877, a new three story brick jail was built for $75,000 next to the courthouse. Each floor had 24 cells, 5 by 8 feet, each having 2 iron cots, one over the other. Each cell had an iron door. The lower floor was designated "Murderers' Row." Judge Parker sentenced 172 men to be hanged, but only 88 were eventually hanged. Of the 88 who were hung, 39 were white, 26 were Indians and 23 were black.

Complaints against outlaws had to be made in person in Fort Smith. So if the complaints were by someone in Indian territory, they might have to travel two hundred miles to file it. Warrants were then sworn out and accumulated before taking them to the U.S. Marshal's office to be served. An estimated 90 percent of the wanted men were murderers, cattle rustlers and horse thieves. The murders may have been committed in a bank robbery or a train robbery or in the process of theft. Many of them already had a reward offered for them. Sometimes, a marshal would arrest someone out in the territory and had to write to the marshal's office to get a writ issued by Judge Parker before bringing them in to the jail.

It was common knowledge that Bass could not read or write before he married Jennie, but he managed to get others to write his letters requesting writs. He would also have someone read him the writs that he was serving. After arresting someone on a writ, he would find someone to identify them to make sure he had arrested the right person. He never arrested the wrong person. Over time, he had a good enough memory that he could identify enough words to be able to do his job. What he lacked in training to read and write, he made up for by his memory. He had never been accused of being stupid. And his wife, Jennie, who had been taught to read and write, was gradually teaching him.

Marshal Boles told Bass: "I have 11 warrants here that need to be served and the parties brought back to Fort Smith, live or dead. I have a warrant for Chub Moore, a white man who killed a negro who raped a white woman, One Eye Hanna, a Creek Indian wanted for murder, Jedick Jackson and John Bruner and Frank Buck, who are colored and wanted for horse thievery, Jim Mack, a Chickasaw, wanted for larceny, John Hoyt, A. Smith, and J. M. McConnell, all whites, and Alex Baker and Daniel Dorsey, Creek Indians, all for introducing. Of course, if you run into anyone else you know is wanted, or the Lighthorse have arrested anyone you want to bring in, we will pay you the fees on them. There is a $1,000 reward each for Jackson, Bruner and Buck."

"All right," Bass told him, "I will get after them as soon as I get a new cook and get all my gear loaded at the livery stable. Frank Pierce will be my posse man on this trip. I don't see needing any more than that."

After finding a cook, Bass hit the long trail to Indian Territory one more time.

3

THE VENDETTA

The gunman came riding into the Washington-McLish Ranch like he had a fire under his saddle. Billy Washington walked out of the house to see what was going on. "Mr. Washington," the gunman blurted out "Bass Reeves has killed the 5 men I was with when we tried to ambush him and he may still be trying to catch me!"

"No," Billy told him, "if he'd wanted to catch you, he would've. Go take that horse to the stables and get that saddle off him, before he dies of a heat stroke." The horse was more important to him than the gunman. Even though it wasn't one of his best horses, it probably cost him $50.

Billy went back into the house raving at the top of his voice, "That damn Bass Reeves!He let that one gunman come back here alive as a warning to us not to mess with him. I'm going to get that son-of-a-bitch killed if it's the last thing I do!"

Dick McLish, his partner in the ranch said "Bass Reeves is a hard man to kill. Many people have tried to kill him and he ended up killing them. He's killed more than 10 men that I know of and some, like our men, probably weren't reported. We don't have anyone working for us that would be capable of killing him. Cherokee Bill would probably be the only guy I know that would even try to kill Bass and he likes Bass, so I don't know if he would even be interested. Ned Christy is another guy who might be able to kill him, but they have some kind of connection. I am thinking we need to find somebody that Bass doesn't even know."

"Well," Billy said, "I'm going to find someone who will kill that son-of-a-bitch if it's the last thing that I do. You can count on that." The next day, Billy rode to Muskogee. The majority of marshals who'd been killed in the line of duty had been killed within a 50 mile radius of Muskogee, which was known as the "Wildest town in the Wild West." When he got to Muskogee, he put up signs that said, "Wanted, Good Gunfighters to protect cattle herd from murderers and thieves. $500 per year. Up to $5 thousand bonus paid for killings. Must apply in person at the Washington-McLish Ranch."

Soon after that, gunfighters started to apply at the ranch. Billy was patient, taking his time to test their skills with a gun and rifle as well as their riding skills. They needed to hire gunmen to replace the ones that Bass had killed, so he would probably hire 6 of the best. Some of the applicants had been in the Confederate army and some had been in the Union army. Some were former lawmen and former Lighthorse. Some were former slaves. Billy didn't care. He wanted to pick out the very best gunmen he could find, regardless of their background.

After he had picked out the best 6 men he could find, he asked them: "Do any of you have a problem facing up to a U.S. Marshal?"

One of the men asked him, "which U.S. Marshal did you have in mind?"

"Bass Reeves," Billy told them, "is someone who is sometimes on the wrong side of the law as far as we're concerned." Three of the men left. The other three, who were from Texas and had fought for the Confederacy, allowed they were willing to do whatever was necessary if the pay was right.

"I pay $500 per year to my gunmen, which is the same money that they pay U.S. Marshals. But for the man who kills Bass Reeves, there'll be a $5,000 reward." The three Texans all seemed pretty excited by that. All of them had killed before, both in the army and afterwards. One of them had been a Texas Ranger and before that, a Union army Colonel. His name was Jake McCullough.

Two of them, Frank Buck and John Bruner, had been making a living selling whiskey to Indians and had been told that Bass Reeves had a warrant out for them for stealing some horses. When they told Billy that the marshal had warrants for them, he seemed pleased. "Does Bass know what you two look like?" Billy asked.

"We don't think so," they replied.

"Good," Billy said, "but he'll find you. You should play along if he talks to you and pretend you'll help him find the men he's looking for. In the meantime, he asked Jake McCullough if he could come up with two more gunmen capable of taking on Bass Reeves. He had a feeling the other two would end up getting killed.

McCullough told him "I've commanded some very good soldiers during the war and have robbed a train with two men who're some of the best gunmen I know. They've been a part of the Dalton gang off and on. I don't think they're running with the Dalton's anymore. I know that Bass Reeves has been after them before and I think they would know him if they saw him. He might not recognize them because they were with the gang when they saw him."

"Can you get in touch with them?" Billy asked.

"I think so," McCullough said, "I believe they're still somewhere around Muskogee. If they are, they'll be in a saloon sooner or later. If I hire them, I want a cut of the $5,000 if one of them kills him."

"If one of them kills him, you can decide who gets the reward." Billy said. McLish later agreed to the plan. He also suggested that someone who worked for them who would not be recognized should go to Bass Reeve's ranch and try to buy three of the best horses he could find for these men to ride. That way, they could either catch him or outrun him if they needed to. Billy thought that was a good plan. "We may have to pay $150 each for a horse from Reeves' ranch," Billy said, "but if we have slower horses, that would be a big disadvantage."

"I agree," McLish said. "If Frank Buck and John Bruner manage to kill Bass, fine, but if not, we'll have a plan in place to finish him once and for all. Which one of our men would be the best one to pick out some good horses and wouldn't be recognized?"

"We should find out when Bass goes out on his next trip and send Fred Cobb up to his ranch." Billy said. He would be the best one.

When Bass headed back out to Indian Territory, Fred Cobb was headed to the marshal's ranch. As Cobb reached the top of the hill, he was stopped by an Indian guard who asked him what his business was at the ranch. "I've come to buy some horses for the Union Army," he said.

"You sure the army has the money to buy horses from Bass Reeves?" the guard asked. "I'm prepared to pay up to $150 per horse in cash, if I find what we want." Cobb said.

"O.K." the guard said, "I'll let you go on up. When you get to the first white house on the right side of the road, that's where you'll find Mr. Saunders. He'll take care of you." Cobb rode on up to the top of the plateau and was absolutely amazed at the beauty of the place. The pastures were immaculate with white picket fences and the stables looked like they were all new. He came to the first white house and knocked on the door and was met by Jane Saunders.

"The guard at the top of the hill told me that this was where I could find Mr. Saunders." Cobb said, "I'm looking to buy some special horses for the Union Army."

"He's out back, chopping some wood," Jane told him "you can have a seat on the porch while I go get him. Would you like some sweet tea to drink?"

"That'd be wonderful," he said.

Jane didn't like the man and told her husband, Green Saunders that when she went to get him. "There's this man out front who says he's here to buy some special horses for the Union Army. I'm getting a bad feeling about him. The army usually sends officers to pick out their own horses when they're buying. And Bass said we weren't selling them any horses we own for $50, which is what they usually try to pay. Something just doesn't seem right."

"I'll go talk to him." Green said.

"Good afternoon," Green said, as Jane handed the man a glass of sweet tea. "My wife tells me you're looking to buy some horses for the army."

"That's correct," Cobb answered, "they've authorized me to pay up to $150 per horse."

"So I guess they've finally decided if they want good horses they're going to have to pay the price? I guess the officers were too stubborn to come up here themselves?" Green asked.

"That's right," Cobb answered "you know how those officers are."

"Sure do," Green responded, "they're pretty arrogant." Even though Green wasn't sure the man could be trusted, he decided he'd go ahead and show him some horses. He guessed if he payed with cash, he didn't have to trust the guy. While Green was showing him around, Cobb stopped at the fenced area that held Bass's personal horses.

"How much for these horses?" Cobb asked.

"Those are not for sale." Green replied.

"Not for any price?" Cobb persisted.

"Not for any price." Green replied, "those are Mr. Reeves' personal horses."

"O.K.," Cobb replied, "do you have any horses that are as good as these that you would sell?"

"We're in the business of selling horses," Green replied, "and I'll show you some that will look just as good to you and are probably just as fast."

"Good." Cobb responded.

Green then took him to a pasture that had all of their best breeding horses that were for sale. Cobb picked out a Pinto, a sorrel and a black horse, that looked a lot like Midnight that Bass rode. It also had a white diamond on its forehead.

"How much do you want for those three horses," Cobb asked.

"Those would run you $150 each." Green said.

Cobb had never paid that much for a horse in his life, but it wasn't his money and he'd been instructed to buy the best horses he could buy. He counted out $450 and handed it to Green.

As he rode down the hill with the horses tied behind him, Cobb thought it would be best to stable them in Fort Smith, since it was going to be dark by the time he got there. He'd get some drinks at the saloon and be on his way the next morning. They were pretty frisky, so he didn't want to deal with them in the dark. Besides, there were too many horse thieves around.

The next day, Cobb went to get the horses. He had also been instructed to find the best and lightest saddles he could find in Fort Smith and have the horses saddled for the trip to the ranch. He worried about running into horse thieves all the way back to the ranch, but the trip was uneventful. He didn't want to have to explain to Billy why he came back without the horses or the money. He knew if he fled, Billy would hunt him down. Billy never gave up on anything. And he knew Billy would never give up on killing Bass Reeves.

By the time Fred Cobb made it back to the Washington-McLish ranch, Jake McCullough had located the two men he had been looking for in Muskogee. Cobb was no sissy himself, but those two guys scared the hell out of him. He hoped they liked the horses. Jake immediately picked out the black horse to ride for himself. He was fond of black shirts and pants and had a special made black holster that held two U.S. Army Colt .45s, with black grips and 6 notches on each handle. Cobb wondered if he had killed 6 men or 12. He didn't dare ask. The other two men picked horses and they all mounted up. They raced to the nearest fence and back. The black horse won every time.

Jake was excited. "I'd like to see Bass Reeves outrun me on this horse. In fact, I'll run Bass Reeves down and catch him with his own horse. That'd be something, wouldn't it boys?"

They all grinned at the thought. It was like watching the devil and his helpers, Cobb thought. They were scary as hell. He was glad he didn't have to share a bunkhouse with them. The gunmen had their own quarters.

The men seemed to be pleased with their horses. They took the horses to the stable and went into the main house to eat dinner.

"Cobb tells us that Bass is over this way collecting prisoners." Billy told McCullough. "Two of the people he has warrants for are working with us. Dick and I think we should see if they can kill him or wound him. We don't think they can kill him, but if they could at least wound him, it would make it easier for you to finish him off.

You should go to Muskogee and meet 'em at the saloon and stay close enough to see what happens. When you see your chance, move in and kill him yourself."

"If we get the chance to kill him first, we're going to do it," Jake said, "I don't plan on sharing any reward with those two."

"That's fine," Billy said, "I'll leave it up to you to figure out when to make your move."

"We'll go into Muskogee tomorrow morning," McCullough said, "and see if we can locate Frank Buck and John Bruner."

After looking for wanted criminals for two weeks, Bass Reeves stopped at Atoka and reported his progress. He dictated a letter to Col. Thomas Boles, U.S. Marshall, in Fort Smith, letting him know of the following captures: One Eye Hanna, Chub Moore, Jedick Jackson, Jim Mack,

John Hoyt, A. Smith, J. M. McConnell, Alex Baker and Daniel Dorsey.

Lighthorse had told him that two men known as Frank Buck and John Bruner were in Muskogee and had been seen at the saloon. So the marshal left the cook and posseman and the prison wagon behind in Atoka and headed to Muskogee.

When Bass got to Muskogee, he rode straight to the saloon and dismounted and walked into the saloon. Most U.S. Marshals were hesitant to walk into a saloon in Muskogee without a posseman or another marshal at their side. Most of the people who frequented the saloons were violent men and the more guns on your side, the better. Bass walked into the saloon and stood at the door and in a booming voice, announced, "I'm Bass Reeves, U.S. Marshal, and I'm looking for a man named Frank Buck and a man named John Bruner. They're both negros who're wanted for horse thievery."

Two colored men stood up and said "We know where those men are, and for $100 each, we'll help you find them. We think they have rewards out for 'em."

"They do have rewards out for 'em," Bass allowed, "and I'll pay you $100 each if you'll lead me to 'em."

"It'll be about two days travel from here," one of the men said, "so we better get started." Bass and the two men left the saloon and he let them lead the way. He sensed that someone might be following them, but could never see anyone. They decided to camp for the night next to a small stream.

Bass had some biscuits with ham between them wrapped up in his saddlebags and shared them with the two other men. He then made some coffee. He did not mind roughing it and he loved his coffee. While he was making the coffee, he noticed that both of the men were acting funny and both kept one hand on their gun. That's a strange way for them to be acting, he thought. He pretended to go around behind one of the men, who was John Bruner, to check on his horse and turned his back to Bruner, but still turning his head where he could keep an eye on him. When he saw that Bruner was slowly drawing his gun, Bass made a quick move behind him and grabbed his gun. When he did, the other man, who was Frank Buck, went for his gun. Bass quickly drew and aimed Bruner's gun and killed Buck with a single shot in the chest. He then promptly tied Bruner's hands behind his back.

"So who are you?" Bass demanded of Bruner.

"I'm John Bruner, please don't kill me."

"Who's the man I just killed?" Bass asked him.

"That was Frank Buck you killed. We was both working for Billy Washington and he paid us to kill you."

"Will you testify to that in Judge Parker's Court?" Bass inquired.

"If you won't kill me, I'll testify to that in court." Bruner said. He figured that would keep the marshal from killing him.

Suddenly, shots were fired and Bass could see the flames jumping off the guns in the dark. Instinctively, he returned fire, aiming at the source of the gunfire and hitting one of the men. The night then went quiet and the fire began to die down, making it dark as well. He supposed if there were any more men, they might wait until he went to sleep and try to kill him or wait until daylight. Bass began to miss having a dog. He could get some sleep if he had Bandit. The dog would wake him if someone approached the camp and if he had a dog, they would not have been able to get up on him in the first place. But he had also been distracted by what happened with the other two men.

He didn't want to try to saddle up the horses and mount the prisoner at night. That might give them another chance to shoot him. He'd not heard them ride away, so he guessed they were waiting for another chance. Having no other choice, he stayed awake all night, between a couple of trees, and let the campfire stay out so they couldn't see him any better than he could see them. He knew there were more men by the distance between the flames from the guns, but he wasn't sure how many.

At daybreak, the gunfire started again, with bullets bouncing off the ground around Bass and his prisoner. The shots were coming from two different directions and they didn't seem to care if they killed his prisoner, as bullets were hitting near him as well.

"They're Billy Washington's men!", Bruner screamed, as a bullet grazed one of his legs. "One's a former Texas Ranger and he was going to bring two of his men. So there are probably two of 'em left."

"That's good to know," Bass shouted, "that'll get you some time off when I get you into Fort Smith."

"You mean if you get me back to Fort Smith!" Bruner shouted.

"I've seen better shots than these two." Bass grunted, taking aim with his .38-40 and dispatching one of the shooters. The other shooter then turned and ran to his horse and then out of sight. "Stay here!" Bass shouted, as he threw his saddle on Midnight and tightened it down.

"Don't worry, I ain't moving!" Bruner screamed.

Bass heard the sound of a horse running as he finally managed to mount Midnight. We will see how fast his horse is, Bass thought to himself. He was pretty sure Midnight would run him down. By the time he was able to see the departing rider, he was probably a thousand yards, or better, in front of Bass.

That was a shot that was too far, even for the .38-40. But Bass had the Winchester in one hand and the reins in the other. He thought the man was going to head to the Washington-McLish ranch, but it looked like he was headed to Texas. Bass was sure he wasn't going to make it. That's a pretty fast horse, he thought. They were staying about the same distance apart, which really surprised Bass. He had never had another horse outrun his.

He followed the man for about 3 miles, until he realized he wasn't gaining on him. The man was riding a black horse that looked familiar, but he couldn't get close enough to know for sure. It was the first time he'd ever had someone escape from him on a horse. He had a hard time believing this had happened and thought he'd better head back to his prisoner. When he got to where the men had tied up their horses, he found two dead men he'd killed and recognized the two horses they'd been riding.

The pinto was a horse he'd bought from a Creek Indian, because it was the finest and fastest pinto he'd ever seen. He guessed the other horse was his black sorrel that looked like Midnight. He wouldn't have guessed the black horse could've gained on Midnight, but he'd been riding Midnight a long way and the black horse may have been better rested. He thought, "what the hell are my three horses doing here?" Then he had a thought that made a chill ran down his spine. What if they'd gone to his ranch and stolen the horses and killed his family?

He had no way of knowing how they got the horses until he got back to Fort Smith. It wasn't until he got back to the camp that he realized one of the bullets had grazed his right calf. He was glad it didn't hit the horse. He would've been hurt worse being pitched off a dead horse than being hit in the calf. He tied a bandana around the wound and started gathering the camp and getting John Bruner on a horse, as well as the dead man, Frank Buck. He decided to mount them on the pinto and the sorrel. He would mount the two dead men from the hill on the two horses that Buck and Bruner were riding. He didn't want the men who'd shot at him on his horses.

He rejoined the cook and posseman at the prison wagon in Atoka. He put Bruner in the prison wagon and tied the dead men to horses. They had about all of the prisoners and dead men they could tend to. It was time to head back to Fort Smith. He was anxious to get back to

Mount Vista and make sure his family was safe. He doubted those men could have made it past his guard and Green Saunders, but he couldn't help but worry. It seemed like someone was trying to kill him and maybe his family. He would have to think about putting a guard at the bottom of the mountain as well as at the top. He thought about that on his way back to Fort Smith.

As they rode into Fort Smith with the 4 dead men on horses trailing the prison wagon with 11 prisoners, even the people who were used to seeing Bass ride in were impressed. His previous biggest "haul" was 17 horse thieves, but this was the first time he'd brought in 4 dead men and 11 prisoners. He'd brought in about $3,000 in rewards and probably about $900 in fees. Plus he got two of his own horses back. Not a bad trip if his family was safe.

After getting the doctor to tend to his wound and to John Bruner, he put Bruner in jail, telling the jailer to keep him separate from the rest of the prisoners. He'd be a valuable witness in Billy Washington's trial.

He was pleased when he rode up the mountain and was greeted by his Indian guard.

"Everything O.K.?" Reeves asked.

"Everything is O.K." the guard replied.

That was music to his ears. He continued to think about adding a guard just in case someone else tried to come on his property who didn't belong. He stopped at Green Saunder's house before he went to see his family. He had his two recovered horses tied behind Midnight.

"Green," Bass began, "I've brought back two horses that belonged to us. The two men that were riding them tried to kill me. I think the man who escaped me was also riding one of our horses."

"Damn!" exclaimed Green, "Jane said she didn't trust that guy!"

"What do you mean?" Bass asked.

"A guy came up here claiming to be buying horses for the army. He picked out the two horses you have and a black horse with a diamond on its forehead, that looked like Midnight."

"Well," Bass said, "that sure explains why I wasn't able to catch him. That is a fast horse. I should have put him with my riding horses and given him a name! I believe he could outrun Midnight, even if Midnight was rested. I made a mistake lettin' that horse get sold."

"Bass," Green continued, "I'm very sorry that I let that man leave here with our horses, but he paid me $450 cash."

Bass laughed that booming laugh of his and said, "Heck, Green, you just sold a horse for $450 since we got two of the horses back. As much as I hate the other guy got away with the black horse, $450 for one horse is a pretty good sale!"

Green was relieved that Bass wasn't mad at him and began to chuckle a little himself, thinking how it'd turned out. Bass was so happy that his family was O.K. that he could overlook anything else. If he'd been there, he probably would've sold those horses for that kind of money, so there was no need to be mad at Green.

Once that matter was settled, Bass headed to his house, eager to see his family again. Green had slaughtered a pig while he was gone and they'd hung it in the smokehouse to cook for several days. By the time Bass got to the house, he could smell the ham that he would be eating for dinner, along with Jennie's black-eyed peas and homemade cornbread. She'd made what some people referred to as "scalded bread" which was made of corn meal and patted into patties by hand and then deep fried. Some people called them corn pones. Bass called them wonderful.

4

BILLY'S PLAN GOES WRONG

Eventually, the word got back to Billy Washington that Bass Reeves killed Frank Buck and captured John Bruner, and he'd also killed the two men that Jake McCullough had hand picked. Not only that, but Jake McCullough had taken off to Texas to get away from Bass, taking the horse that Billy paid $150 for! And on top of that, Bass had captured the other two horses that Billy had paid $150 each for! He was so mad, he looked like he was going to explode. Billy was about 5 foot, 8 inches tall and resembled Napoleon Bonaparte. He was short and mean as a snake. He hated tall people like Bass Reeves who could look down at him.

Billy sent for Fred Cobb.

"Cobb," Billy started, "do you think there's any way we could get on top of Mount Vista and kill Bass Reeve's family? If I can't kill that son-of-a-bitch, then I'll kill his whole damn family!"

Cobb thought about that for a second or two before answering. He knew he didn't want any part of this plan. He knew if someone killed Bass Reeves' family, they'd better leave the country or he would hunt them down. Maybe Billy was just talking to blow off steam.

"Mr. Washington, nobody challenged me until I got to the top of the mountain. There was only one Indian they had standing a guard position at the top of the hill. You couldn't see him until he'd already got you in his sights and challenged you. I suspect if a whole group of people came up that mountain road that weren't wearing army uniforms, they'd get shot before they got to the top."

"Well, what if they were wearing army uniforms?" Billy asked.

"Well," Cobb continued, "that man Green Saunders, who runs the ranch, told me that usually the officers come up to pick out their own rides. He was a little suspicious that I didn't have army officers with me when I bought those horses."

"So we'd need to get hold of some army officer uniforms?" Billy asked.

"Probably," Cobb said.

About that time, McLish, who had been sitting in on the conversation said, "I think I know where we can get a couple of army uniforms."

"The other problem that we have, is that after they kill his family, they'll have to go back through Fort Smith." Billy said, "If anybody finds out about what happened, they will send every U.S. Marshal in Fort Smith after them. If we could get some Mexicans to do it, they could head South back towards Mexico and escape before anyone knew what happened."

"I think we need to hire some more Texas gunmen to do it," McLish said, "then they can go South to Texas or Mexico when it's done. We still have people coming in that have read our signs in Muskogee. Most of the people showing up here are murderers anyway. They'd kill anyone for money. And we still have the money. We were out only a month's wages and $450 for horses. The people who kill Reeves' family won't need to outrun him, so a regular horse will do. I think we can get some uniforms for about $100 each. It shouldn't take more than 3 or 4 men to kill his family."

"Let's do it," Billy said.

Fred Cobb thought that was a bad idea that would come back on them in a bad way and said so to one of the Creek Indians who worked for him. The Creek Indian knew Bass's wife, Jennie, who was raised as a Creek. The next day he was gone. Cobb began to worry about telling the Indian what was going on, but decided to keep quiet about it. He knew Billy would probably shoot him if he knew that he may've jeopardized the plan.

Two days later, the Creek Indian guard at the top of the Mount Vista trail saw a rider approaching from the bottom of the trail. When the rider got to the top of the hill, the guard challenged him: "Who are you and why are you coming up this trail?"

The man answered in the Creek language: "I'm John Redbird and I'm a Creek Indian and I need to talk to Mr. Bass Reeves if he's here."

The guard responded back to him in Creek: "Mr. Reeves is here and I'll take you to him." The two rode to the Reeves residence together, with the guard sending a replacement back to cover his post.

As they approached the house, they could see Bass sitting on the porch, smoking his pipe in his over-sized rocking chair. "Mr. Bass," the guard said, "this man is John Redbird, a Creek Indian, who's come to see you."

Bass responded in Creek: "Welcome, John Redbird, what can I do for you?"

John responded back to him in Creek "I have come from the Washington-McLish ranch near Muskogee and I'm afraid the owners have a plan to kill your family."

Bass jumped up out of his rocking chair and said, "What? Where did you hear this?"

The Indian responded in Creek: "Fred Cobb, who's the man that came up here to buy horses while pretending to be with the army, told me that Billy Washington and Dick McLish plan to dress some gunmen in Union Army officer uniforms and ride up to Mount Vista and kill your family the next time you're out working in the Indian Territory."

"Do you know who the gunmen are?" Bass asked.

"They haven't hired them yet," the Indian responded, "but they have signs up in Muskogee trying to recruit more gunmen. You've killed or captured almost everyone they've hired so far."

Now Bass was really mad. He could take care of himself out in the territory, but he couldn't be home protecting his family all the time. He thought about asking for a warrant on Billy Washington, with John Bruner, the gunman he had captured, and the Indian, providing the testimony.

"Why are you telling me this?" Bass asked the Indian.

"I know your wife, Jennie," he said, "and we're friends. I also know you're a friend of the Creek Indian. Billy Washington speaks with forked tongue and treated me badly."

Bass had spoken to the Indian in Creek to be sure of who he was. He was sure the man was telling the truth.

"I appreciate you telling me about this," Bass said, "and if my wife verifies that you were friends in the past, I'd like to hire you. I've been planning to hire someone, because I think we need a guard at the bottom of the hill. The Indians I have working here are all Creek, so you won't have any trouble communicating with them."

"It'd be my honor to work for you, Mr. Reeves," the Indian said, "Those people I've been working for have dark souls."

It wasn't time for Bass to hit the trail again, but he mounted Rusty the next morning to go into Fort Smith. He wanted to talk to Marshal Boles and get advice about what to do.

"Colonel Boles," Bass begun, "I have a situation that I'm not sure how to handle and I need your advice."

"What kind of problem do you have Bass?" Boles responded.

"Well," Bass continued, "I'm fairly sure that Billy Washington and Dick McLish have sent gunmen to try to kill me. As you know, I just had to kill two men that they sent and arrested the third man, John Bruner. Bruner told me he'd testify in court that Washington and McLish hired him to kill me. Not only that, but I've just found out that they may be trying to hire someone to kill my whole family."

"Well," Boles responded, "if they're crazy enough to come over to this side of the river and try something like that, we'll kill them all and go to their ranch and arrest the ones that're still alive, if it takes every marshal we have. I'm not sure if we want to swear out a warrant on Billy where we only have a murderer and Indian as a witness. I think you should go talk to Judge Parker about this."

Bass walked into Judge Parker's office and the judge looked up smiling. "Got some time for more law book lessons?" the judge asked him.

"No sir, Judge, I've come to ask you for some advice." Bass answered.

The judge asked, "What can I help you with Bass, you look awfully serious?"

"Well sir," Bass continued, "I've reason to believe that Billy Washington and Dick McLish have sent people to try and kill me. They sent one of their men to my ranch, pretending to be a buyer for the army, and bought 3 of my finest horses. The next thing I know, I'd killed two men who were riding my horses who were trying to kill me. A third man outran me towards Texas. He was on a black horse that was bought at my ranch. I had to kill one man and arrest another who said that Billy had offered them a $5,000 reward to kill me, and the man I arrested will testify to that."

"You've got to be kidding me," the judge interrupted, "they have the gall to send men to try to kill one of my marshals! I'm going to issue a writ right now for Billy Washington and Dick McLish! I'll have this witness brought up to my office right away to verify the story."

"Thank you judge," Bass said, "but it gets even worse. A Creek Indian came to our place and told me that Washington and McLish intend to hire some gunmen to put on Union Army uniforms and ride to my place while I'm gone and kill my family." Bass thought the judge was going to explode. He'd never seen the judge this mad.

"Right now, I really wish I'd allow myself to curse!" Judge Parker said "I have a bunch of words I would like to use to describe those low-life outlaws who're supposed to be prominent citizens in the territory. Can you get that Indian to come over and swear what he heard?"

"Well," your honor, Bass said, "he got the information second hand from a man named Fred Cobb, who's the same man who came to my place and pretended to buy horses for the army. Billy asked him how hard it would be to come up our mountain without getting shot at."

"Well," the judge said, "I still want to talk to that Indian. Get him to come by here. We may not be able to swear out a writ on Billy, but maybe we can lay a trap for his men. If we can get one more of his men and the Indian to testify in this case, we may be able to get Billy and maybe McLish hanged or at least put in prison in Detroit. That's the worst prison they could be sent to. Have you spoken to Marshal Boles about this?"

"Yessir," Bass said, "and he told me to come talk to you."

"Would you be able to come back to Fort Smith tomorrow?" the judge asked.

"Yessir," Bass said, "I could be here as early as you need me."

"Let's have lunch brought to the courtroom tomorrow," the judge said, " where I can talk to all of the marshals that are available, as well as Marshal Boles."

"Yessir," Bass said, "I'll be there."

The next morning when Bass arrived in the courtroom, he saw that the judge had several marshals sitting in the jury section. U.S. Marshal deputies J.H. Mershon, William P. Pittcock, Bud Kell and Heck Thomas were all present, along with Marshal Boles. Mershon was short and stocky, Pittcock was tall and thin and Bud Kell and Heck Thomas were of medium build and height. All were somber men, but all except Mershon still had a sense of humor.

"Men," Judge Parker began, "it has come to my attention that there is a plot by Billy Washington and his partner, Dick McLish, to disguise some men as Union Army officers, who plan to go to Mount Vista and pretend to want to buy some horses from Bass."

"Once they are up on the mountain, they plan to kill Bass's whole family, Green Saunders and everyone who works for him who gets in the way. Billy has offered a $5,000 reward to the people who would do this. He has a signs up in Muskogee, offering to hire gunmen for his ranch.

When they come looking for a job, he intends to hire the best men he can find who'd be willing to do this. We all know the territory is full of men who would kill anyone for that much money. I found out all of this by talking to a Creek Indian who'd been working at the Washington-McLish ranch. He now works for Bass."

The marshals were clearly disturbed about what Billy and Dick had planned. They had seen some bad things happen in their days in law enforcement, but this was the first time they knew about a man's family being targeted. It made them uncomfortable, as all of them except Mershon had families. All had worked with Bass at one time or another and some had sent for him when they got into prolonged shootouts because he was such a good shot. He'd helped them out when they needed him, so they were all willing to help.

"This is something we need to do," Judge Parker said, "I want every marshal in this room to go to Bass's ranch beforehand, one at a time, to avoid attention, and stay there.

Next week, when Bass is due to hit the trail again, we'll have marshal Rufus Cannon, a negro who can be disguised to look like Bass, ride out with Bass's cook, posse and prison wagon. Anyone who sees him will think it's Bass leaving town.

I want Rufus to leave from your ranch, Bass, wearing your pistol belt and Colt .45s and riding that red sorrel that you usually ride. I want him to be wearing one of your suits or one just like it. He's almost as big as you. I also want you to let him wear that big black hat that you usually wear. But you can hang on to that .38-40 Winchester of yours because you will probably need it.

I would hate to be the men who are coming to your ranch.

Bass, I think the Creek Indian who worked for Washington-McLish should be at the bottom of the hill and signal the top Indian when he sees the men coming. I am sure they have some kind of whistle they can use as a signal and I want the marshals to be ready behind Green Saunders' house when they get there.

Is there anyone who disputes this plan?" There were none.

"Marshal Boles will stay here in Fort Smith," Judge Parker allowed, "you won't need him and I need for him to start preparing warrants. Bass, I hope you have enough food to feed all of these men for a week."

"Yes sir," Bass answered, "our smoke house is full of ham and turkey and we have more than enough eggs from our chickens. Our garden is producing more tomatoes than we can eat. I think we can move some of our horses to the lower pastures to make room for all of the extra horses. Any man who helps out on this can pick out one of my best horses to take with you when you leave." There were big smiles on the marshal's faces. They all were riding horses they'd bought from Bass. He always gave them a good discount, but free was better.

"You can all camp out," Bass said, "like you do all of the time, but if it rains, you can bunk on our porch. There's plenty of room. There's also a bunkhouse where the ranch hands stay and there are plenty of bunks, if you prefer to sleep there."

Most of the marshals had been to the ranch to buy horses and some had eaten at the ranch. Jennie had always made sure they were welcomed. Most were looking forward to eating her cooking. Later, one by one, they started going up to the ranch and Bass was there to greet them. He took Rufus Cannon to his sister's house, so she could make finishing touches and make sure the suit she made for him would fit. He was pretty pleased to get the suit at no charge. A suit like that would normally cost $100. He'd never had the urge to wear a suit before, but he thought it made him look special. The black hat that Bass usually wore fit him well and looked good also. He might have to buy himself one later on.

When it was time for him to go, Bass handed Rufus his pistol belt with the two Colt .45s facing butt forward.

"You think you can draw these pistols backwards like I do?" he asked Rufus.

"It'll take some practice, I'm sure. But I guess I'll have plenty of time to do that. I'll have to just vanish once I'm in the Indian Territory... We just want 'em to think you've left Fort Smith. Someone is probably watchin' for you to leave."

"Probably so. It's usually no secret when I leave," Bass said "some people count down the days I'm gone, so they'll know when I get back, just so they can see how many men I've killed."

"Yeah," Rufus said, "they don't usually pay that much attention to me, because I try to stay out of trouble if possible. I don't go after those big rewards like you do, because those're usually the most dangerous men. Low risk, no reward... that's me."

"You don't have as many mouths to feed," Bass joked, "just look at all these people up here I have to feed and all these horses."

"Yeah," Rufus joked, as he looked around, "I can see you really need the money."

About that time, Green Saunders showed up with Rusty all saddled up and ready to go. The saddles that Bass owned were pretty easy to identify as well as his horses and pistols. Most people would believe that Rufus was Bass, especially with a handkerchief across the bottom of his face. Bass usually used one to keep from breathing dust when he was riding. Rufus suited up and began to wonder if he could keep the sorrel after all this was over. Rusty was much better than the $50 horses he usually rode.

Rufus began his journey and rode through Fort Smith, down Garrison Road, and turned to the courthouse to pick up his posseman, cook and prison wagon and crossed the river into Indian Territory. He had told the cook and posseman that Bass was ill. As far as he knew, everyone in town thought he was Bass Reeves and he made it a point to sit straight and proud in the saddle.

Meanwhile, back at the ranch, the marshals sat down to a hearty meal Jennie had fixed. She enjoyed showing off her cooking skills and always made people feel welcome at her dinner table. Even Judge Parker was known to wander by to share a meal when he had a spare moment. He had very few spare moments, but he would come by at least once a month to get his fill. He was addicted to Jennie's pecan pie, filled with fresh pecans from the pecan orchard on the ranch. Her fried peach pies, with fresh peaches from the peach orchard on the ranch, were pretty darn good too!

The marshals discussed their plan and decided it would be best to let the men come all the way up the hill and up to Green Saunders' house before they confronted them. If they all stepped from behind the house at the same time, maybe they could capture them without a fight. The more live witnesses against Washington and McLish, the better.

Back at the Washington-McLish ranch, they were making their own plans. They had tested 10 men so far and had finally eliminated all but 5 for the task at hand and would keep a few more to stay at the ranch. Billy then gathered the 5 men they had chosen in front of the main ranch house and asked:

"Is there any one of you who would refuse to kill women and children for a $5,000 reward?" He asked. All the men answered "No."

"We're willing to pay you $5,000 that can be split among you when the job is finished. We'll pay you $500 each up front and once the job is finished and you return to Texas, we'll send you the rest of the money. The job will be to ride to Van Buren, Arkansas, to the top of Mount Vista and kill everyone who's up there… Any questions?"

"Will there by anyone with guns when we get there?" one man asked.

"There is an Indian guard who'll be at the top of the hill with a rifle. But we're going to provide you with Union Army officer's uniforms and they'll think you're coming up the mountain to buy horses. They should let you ride up the hill without any trouble. If they happen to shoot at you coming up the hill, you'll know that something is wrong and you can turn around and escape. Once you get to the top of the hill, you can proceed to the houses and carry out your business. The only man you might have to fight with a gun would be Green Saunders, who runs the ranch, and an Indian or two. This ranch belongs to Marshal Bass Reeves, but we have word he's already left on about a two week trip to the Indian Territory. Any questions?"

"So Bass Reeves won't be there?" One man asked.

"He'll be gone." Billy said.

"Are you sure of that?" The man asked.

"We're sure," Billy assured him "one of our men saw him leaving Fort Smith yesterday morning."

"I sure wouldn't want to go up there if Bass Reeves was up there," the man said.

"I understand," Billy said, "he'll be 30 miles away by tomorrow. By the time you get to Van Buren, he'll be near Muskogee."

"Some of you are probably on his list to arrest." Billy said. "You'll be better off where you'll be, killing his family."

That made sense to them. And they would be $5,000 richer and could go down to Mexico and live a long and prosperous life with that kind of money. Bass wouldn't bother them there.

"Also," Billy continued, "Reeves has got $1,000 worth of the finest horses you'll ever see, up there at his house, according to Fred Cobb, who scouted the place out. Fred says that Green Saunders lives in the first white house on the right side of the road. The rest of the family will be in the other two houses. The biggest log house is where you'll find Reeves' wife and children."

He gave them a map that Fred Cobb had drawn showing how to get up the mountain and where the buildings were located.

"What you need to do is ride to Fort Smith and stay in a hotel overnight. Then you can change into uniforms and slip out of town early in the morning and go to Van Buren."

The men agreed and were on their way. They each had $500 in their pocket and had plans to have a good time while they were in Fort Smith. They briefly discussed just taking the money they had and leaving. But the idea of taking some of Bass Reeve's high dollar horses was very tempting, so they decided they would do what they were told to do. Even if the $5,000 reward didn't get to them for some reason, they'd still have $500 each and some very valuable horses. According to what Fred Cobb had told them, Bass didn't believe in branding his horses, so they'd be easy to sell or trade.

After spending the night in Fort Smith, the men met at the edge of town and changed into their uniforms, so they wouldn't attract any attention. It was about five miles to Van Buren and they would have to cross the river again. It was late in the morning when they rode up the hillside to Mount Vista.

At the top of the hill, they were questioned by the Indian guard. They asked him to escort them to the stables to look at some horses, so he accompanied them to the first white house, which was Green Saunders'. At the house, the Indian went into the front door and all of a sudden, 5 U.S. Marshals stepped from behind the house, with cocked pistols in their hands, except for Bass, who had his rifle. "Drop them guns! U.S. Marshals!" William Pittcock commanded. The men were so shocked, they drew their guns instinctively and the gunfight was on. The outlaws were no match for the marshals, especially since the marshals already had their guns in their hands. The outlaws drew their guns immediately, but some didn't even clear their holsters before they were hit by the marshal's bullets. Only 2 of the hired gunmen managed to get off a hurried volley of shots.

After a short but furious gun battle, the gunmen were all dead. One was hanging from the stirrup of his horse as his horse ran down the road, kicking him every few steps until the horse was stopped by the Indian guard. The marshals had hoped the men would surrender, so they'd have witnesses against Billy Washington and Dick McLish, but that didn't happen. There was smoke hanging in the air like small clouds that gradually faded away. Their ears were ringing from the loud gunfire and the scent of gunpower was thick in the air.

The marshals surveyed the men to see if they were familiar or if any of them survived. They identified two men who had $500 rewards on them, but couldn't identify the rest. Each man still had a considerable amount of cash in his pocket. They figured that would be money paid by Billy Washington, but couldn't prove it. They found a map in one of the men's pocket that showed how to get to Mount Vista and the location of the buildings on top. The marshals knew that Fred Cobb had been the only one of Washington's men to go to the ranch, but had no way of proving he made the map.

One of the men rode a horse with the Washington-McLish brand on it, but Washington and McLish could say it'd been stolen. Only one of the marshals, William P. Pittcock, suffered a bullet wound. He was hit in his right arm, but it didn't hit the bone. Jennie wrapped a bandage around his arm before they left for Fort Smith. Pittcock would go see the doctor later. It wasn't the first time he'd been shot.

Before the marshals headed out, Bass took them to his stables to pick out their horses. He even let them pick from his personal horses, with the exception of Silver. They took the saddles off the outlaw's horses and put them onto their new horses and tied the dead outlaws on them. Bass would take the outlaw's horses and guns to town later to sell and pay for the outlaws to be buried. Later, he would let Rufus keep Rusty, the horse he usually rode.

This would leave Bass short of horses, so he thought about making a trip to find replacements. Meanwhile, he saddled "Midnight" and would ride him for a while. He would be glad to get his 6-guns back from Rufus...He felt naked without them.

It was quite a scene when the 5 U.S. Marshals came riding down Garrison Road in Fort Smith, as each one of them had a dead man trailing behind them on a horse. The people in town were used to seeing one marshal ride in with a cook wagon and a prison wagon. When more than one marshal left town or returned to town at one time, it was usually when they were after someone like the Dalton Gang. The townspeople met them in the street asking, "Is that the Dalton Gang? Is that the Story Gang? Is that the Glass Gang?" The marshals kept riding straight to Judge Parker's court. They wanted to tell the judge his plan had worked, except for taking prisoners alive.

Judge Parker was pleased, even though he had hoped some men could be captured alive. He said, "This should put a stop to this nonsense by Billy Washington and Dick McLish. They would be crazy to continue a vendetta against Bass after this. I'm going to swear out a writ on Billy and Dick and I want every one of you marshals to go with Bass to serve it. William, you probably need to stay here and let the doctor look at that arm."

"Judge," Pitcock said, "I wouldn't want to miss the look on Billy and Dick's face when we arrest them. The arm will be fine. Jennie already tended to it and I'll get the doc to look at it before we leave."

"We'll bring them in," Judge Parker said, "even if we may not be able to get a jury to convict them. That'll serve notice on them that their behavior will not be tolerated by this court. Ordinarily, I wouldn't waste tax money to try someone I wasn't sure we could convict, but this case warrants strong action."

After they got the warrants from Judge Parker, all 5 marshals, including Bass, headed to the Washington-McLish ranch. They knew there were 45 cowboys working at the ranch and maybe 5 to 10 gunmen, so they figured arresting Billy and Dick would be risky. The marshals figured the 45 cowboys would be tending to livestock and wouldn't be a threat to them. They knew they were capable of handling the gunmen and would kill them all if it were necessary. It depended on how Billy and Dick reacted. Would they fight? Would they run? Or would they surrender? The marshals wouldn't know the answer until they got there.

5

Parker Strikes Back

Armed with Warrants for the arrest of Billy Washington and Dick McLish, Deputy U.S. Marshals Bass Reeves, J.H. Mershon, William P. Pittcock, Bud Kell and Heck Thomas rode down Garrison Avenue through Fort Smith and headed towards Indian Territory. It was clear to the people in Fort Smith that something big was going down. There was very little talk about the men that had been brought in dead. Many suspected the events might be connected. There was a rumor in town they were going after Washington and McLish, but it was just a rumor. The marshals would have to spend several days on the trail, so they'd brought Reeves' cook and wagon.

They would either camp in the open or sleep in tents if it rained. They brought a prison wagon, just in case they needed to arrest more of the men at the ranch, if they resisted. It would also be easier to haul dead men in the prison wagon.

After a long trip, the marshals approached the Washington-McLish property. They decided to leave the cook and cook wagon outside the property line, but took the prison wagon with them. The property was thousands of acres and it was more than ten miles from the edge of the property to the main ranch house, where Billy and Dick lived. Before they got to the main house, they were approached by a group of cowboys who were interested in who they were. The cowboys offered no resistance and pointed out the way to the main house. After the encounter, one of the cowboys circled around them at a fast gallop, to warn the others at the ranch that marshals were on the way. The marshals paused to discuss their approach.

"Men," Bass began, "I figure when we get close to the ranch house, we may get shot at with rifles as soon as we're in range. If that happens, we can get behind the prison wagon or lay down so we're a smaller target. Or they may wait until we're really close. There are some water troughs about 50 yards from the main house. If we can reach those troughs, we can set up behind them and the prison wagon. Or they may stay outside and let us ride right up to them, thinking they can outdraw us. Or they could just surrender. I'm hoping they choose to surrender."

Once the marshals were in sight of the main ranch house, they noticed rifles sticking out of windows of the bunkhouse and the upstairs windows of the main ranch house. They pulled their rifles and rode to the water troughs about 50 yards from the main house. Bass, who probably had the loudest voice, shouted, "Billy Washington and Dick McLish, we have warrants for your arrest for attempted murder issued by Judge Isaac C. Parker in Fort Smith. Either come out with your hands up or prepare to die!"

"How do we know you're not just going to kill us, without giving us a chance?" Billy shouted out.

"We ain't shooting at you yet," Bass said, "If we'd wanted to kill you, we would've already done that." The marshals had already dismounted and had taken positions behind the water troughs and the prison wagon.

About that time, 25 cowboys came riding in past the marshals and up to the main house. Billy Washington had sent for them, figuring they would be better potential witnesses than the killers he usually hired for gunmen. The cowboys scattered out, with some of them going into the main house. None of them had guns in their hands.

"We're going to come out with our hands up," Billy shouted, "don't you shoot us, we got all these cowboys who're witnesses."

"We don't plan on shooting at you," Bass hollered back, "just come on out."

Billy and Dick came out of the ranch house with their hands up, along with the 5 gunmen they had hired. Pittcock tied up Billy and Dick and mounted them on horses provided by the ranch hands, and told the gunmen to go back into the house. Billy asked them not to make he and Dick ride in the prison wagon because that would've been humiliating.

The plan to return to Fort Smith was to head west from the ranch to the Arkansas River and then to follow the Arkansas River from there back to Fort Smith. On the second day of the trip they were getting close to the Canadian River crossing, where it ran into the Arkansas River from the south. As they slowed down to cross the Canadian, shots were fired from a hill to their south. J.H. Mershon was hit and knocked from his horse. His horse kept running and crossed the river. It was headed home.

Bass had a bullet pass directly in front of his face and his horse reared up and almost fell over backwards onto him. He drew his rifle after the horse settled back down and scanned the hills. William Pittcock's horse was shot and he tumbled to the ground with the horse. He was able to fetch his rifle and also turn his attention to the hills. Bud Kell and Heck Thomas both drew their rifles from their scabbords and returned fire at the hills. All of the marshals began to fire at the gunmen on the hill. It looked like there were five of them and Bass began to regret not arresting the gunmen at the ranch. He knew it was them on the hill.

Meanwhile, Billy and Dick's horses were headed back towards their ranch. Bass decided to go after them, since he had the fastest horse. It took him about a mile to catch them and get the horses reins tied to his saddle. He was mad about what had happened.

"Dang you," Bass said to Billy and Dick, "I ought to kill both of you right here for trying to escape. Nobody would blame me, if I did."

"We didn't know anyone was going to shoot at us." Billy swore.

"He's telling the truth." McLish said.

"Well, I can tell you one thing," Bass said, "you two are riding in the prison wagon from here to Fort Smith. I don't plan on having to chase you down a second time. I'm sure those men shooting at us are the same 5 gunmen you had at the ranch."

"We didn't tell 'em to do it." Billy said.

"It doesn't matter," Bass said, "you're still riding the rest of the way in the prison wagon."

By the time Bass got back to where the other marshals were, the gunfire had stopped.

"What happened after I left?" Bass asked.

"We chased those men who shot at us," Bud Kell said "and managed to kill two of 'em. We threw 'em in the prison wagon."

"How's J.H.?" Bass asked.

"He's doing fine," Heck Thomas answered. "He just caught a bullet in his upper leg, but we don't think it hit any bone. We tied a rag around it and he can ride in the front of the prison wagon, with the driver. We caught the dead men's horses and tied them to the prison wagon."

"Well," Bass said, "I'm gonna take these two off their horses and put 'em in the prison wagon with the dead men. I hope it stinks in there by the time we get to Fort Smith."

"Come on Bass," Billy complained, "don't put us in the prison wagon."

"I'm not going to have to chase you down again," Bass said, "so you're going in the wagon. That's that."

After tying the horses that Billy and Dick were riding to the prison wagon, the men continued their journey to Fort Smith.

When they arrived in Fort Smith, they drew a pretty large crowd. Billy and Dick were well known around Fort Smith and were considered to be prominent people. There was surprise at their arrest. And most were shocked to see them locked in the prison wagon with two dead men. J.H. Mershon was taken to the town doctor who properly bandaged his wound and confirmed the bullet did no damage to any bones.

Judge Parker didn't want to put Washington and McLish in jail, so he set an immediate hearing for them when they arrived. He figured they had been humiliated enough, after being forced to ride to Fort Smith in a prison wagon. Bass had explained why they'd been put into the wagon and Judge Parker agreed on that decision.

The court room was full of people by the time the plea hearing was convened. The judge had the bailiff bring Billy and Dick both to stand in front of him and they were sworn in to testify.

"You men have charges against you that you hired gunmen to kill Bass Reeves and we have a witness who can testify to that. We also have witnesses who can testify that you hired men to go to Marshal Reeves' house and try to kill his family. How do you men plead to those charges?"

"Well," Billy said, "your honor, we certainly did no such thing! We haven't had a chance to hire a lawyer, but we'll certainly plead not guilty... Marshal Reeves is an outlaw himself and we think we can prove that in court."

"All I asked you to do was say whether or not you plead guilty!" Judge Parker barked, "If you come in here making accusations against my marshals, I will hold you in contempt of court and throw you in the jail below this courthouse and let you rot there until your trial!"

"Sorry, Judge," Billy apologized, "I plead not guilty."

"What about you, McLish?" Judge Parker barked.

"I plead not guilty, your honor." McLish responded.

Neither of them dared to say another word. They could tell the judge was mad. They realized they'd made a mistake trying to kill Bass Reeves. They wondered who the witnesses would be. Had the marshal managed to capture the men they sent to kill Reeves' family? Had the men killed any of Reeves' family? They had no idea what the situation was. They had not heard from any of the men since they had left to go to Mount Vista.

"Let the record show the defendants have pleaded not guilty to attempted murder." Judge Parker said. "The defendants, having considerable property under the jurisdiction of this court are going to be released with the condition that their considerable property is going to be a bond to assure they will show up in court. If they fail to show up for court for any reason, their property will be seized by this court and auctioned at a U.S. Marshal's sale on the steps of this courthouse. Do the defendants understand?"

"What if we get sick or something," Billy asked, "what would happen to our property if that happened?"

"If, for any reason," Parker continued, "you do not show up on your assigned court date, your property will be seized and sold. Understood?"

"Understood, your honor," the two mumbled.

"Your court appearance will be 30 days from now," Judge Parker said, "in this courtroom at 9:00 in the morning. Be here!"

"Yessir," both men said together. They felt like they had just been spanked in public. Both men were angry, but figured this feud with Bass Reeves wasn't worth losing all the property they had worked for, or ending up in prison. It was a sobering thought. After they were released, they went to stay the hotel to get some drinks and entertainment.

"Billy," McLish said, sitting in the saloon, "I must've been an idiot to let you talk me into this vendetta of yours."

"I must have been an idiot to try killing that guy," Billy admitted. "But I'm going to get even with Bass Reeves somehow. You can count on that."

At the saloon, Billy and Dick ran into Bart Simms. Bart Simms owned the *Fort Smith Weekly Elevator*. Of course, Bart wanted to know everything that happened between them and Bass Reeves.

"Did you really try to have Bass Reeves killed?" Simms asked.

"Of course not," Billy said, "we don't know where those men came from or where they got the horses they were riding. Whoever said we did that is a damn liar. You know that Bass Reeves killed our ranch manager, Jim Webb. He killed another of our men when he arrested Webb the first time. He's a natural born killer and he's out of control and everyone knows it. Judge Parker just lets him do anything he wants, even killing his own camp cook. Why isn't he going to trial for that? It doesn't look like Judge Parker's gonna' make him stand trial. But he sends marshals out to arrest us, because he thinks we tried to kill his pet negro."

"That's just not right," Bart Simms told Billy, "and I'm going to make sure everyone in Fort Smith hears your side of the story. Of course, I don't know how long I can keep doing that," looking at Billy to see how he was reacting, "as my newspaper is in financial distress."

"Why's your newspaper in trouble?" Billy asked.

"I suffered some gambling losses and had to put the newspaper up as collateral." Simms answered.

"How much money do you owe?" Billy asked.

"I borrowed $1,000." Simms said.

"How much would it take to make you well?" Billy asked.

"Well, if I had $1,500, that would put me in the clear for at least the next year." Simms answered.

"If we give you the money, would you make sure our story's told in your newspaper?" Billy asked.

"Absolutely." Simms said, "and I won't let up until Bass Reeves gets what's coming to him!"

Billy had a big sinister grin on his face. He thought he'd just made a deal with the devil. "We'll give you the money tomorrow morning after the bank opens." Billy said.

An article appeared in the *Weekly Elevator* the next day that read:

Prominent Landowners Arrested

"Billy Washington and Dick McLish, two hard working, honest men, who are the prominent owners of the Washington-McLish ranch in Indian Territory were arrested this week by Deputy Marshal Bass Reeves and other marshals on a false charge of attempted murder, without allowing them to establish their innocence and dragged around for days in a wagon on the way to Fort Smith, at the same time knowing, as they must have known, that there was no foundation for a case against them. Washington is a man apparently fifty years of age and is recognized by his neighbors as a law abiding citizen, yet Reeves and his men went to his house and handcuffed him like a desperado in the presence of his cowboys.

McLish, who is about forty-five, is also recognized by his neighbors as a law abiding citizen and a prominent Indian. Reeves treated him with like disrespect and handcuffed him in front of his cowboys. This case was evidently trumped up on them by designing men for a purpose, and we understand this might allow people to steal their cattle or horses while they are not there to see after them. Now we protest against all such proceedings by deputy marshals and we are satisfied Col. Boles will not tolerate such capers on the part of his subordinates if the facts are brought properly before him."

Judge Parker was furious when he read the story in the *Weekly Elevator* and sent Marshal Boles to fetch Bart

Simms to his office. Simms was scared to death when he was brought to Judge Parker's office by Marshal Boles.

"Bart Simms," Judge Parker growled "what in God's name are you thinking about, running that blasted article about Bass Reeves and my marshals arresting Billy Washington and Dick McLish? You know what you wrote isn't true! Those men were serving warrants that I issued for their arrests. We have credible witnesses who will testify that they tried to have Bass Reeves and his family killed!"

"Well, Judge," Simms said, "you know there are two sides to every story and I was told my story by Billy Washington and Dick McLish in person. They have the right to tell their story."

"You ought to check on your facts before you start printing garbage like that," Judge Parker angrily told him, "these marshals have a dangerous life already, without you stirring up public anger with a story like this."

"That's my story," Simms said, "and I'm sticking to it!"

"Fine," Judge Parker said, "but I'm warning you that if you continue to print such gossip about my marshals, I shall have you before this court on a contempt of court charge. Think about that before you print any more stories like this!" Simms did not reply, but just sat staring at the judge. He knew Parker was just bluffing. He knew that his newspaper carried a lot of influence.

Simms needed the $1,500 and wasn't sorry about what he'd done. He'd find any piece of dirt he could find on Bass Reeves and print the story any time he felt like it. After a brief stare-down, Judge Parker told him to leave. Maybe next time, Simms thought, Judge Parker would be more forthcoming with news of arrests they were about to make. Maybe Judge Parker would be inclined to tell his side of the story first.

The judge was thinking about what an idiot Simms was, thinking he could take on the law enforcement system that had been set up by President Ulysses S. Grant himself. He had often been misrepresented by the press, both in the past, as a Congressman from Missouri, and as a judge. It had been said by the press that he was opposed to the right of appeal. That was untrue, but he was opposed to irresponsible journalism. He had been called heartless and bloodthirsty by the press; however he always told a jury "Permit no innocent man to be punished, but let no guilty man escape."

6

Belle Starr

Because of the stress from worrying about his family, Judge Parker told Bass to take a couple of weeks off. He rarely took a vacation, but welcomed the time off as an opportunity to go somewhere and find replacement horses for his personal use. He knew there was only one other person in the Indian Territory who loved horses more than he did and that was Belle Starr.

Born as Myra Belle Shirley, in 1846, in Carthage, Missouri, she was about 39 years old now and had been through a lot of turmoil. Though widely referred to as a "Bandit Queen," Belle had been born and raised by a sophisticated and wealthy family and could be charming when she wanted to be. She was born the daughter of a judge. Her father had owned slaves and was on the Confederate side of the war.

Belle had always loved to ride horses and as a teenager would ride horses in places a woman should not have been. She was thrilled by getting chased by bad men, but never got caught by them. She always had expensive horses. She even became a carrier of messages during the Civil War and once was charged as a spy by the Union Army.

Her association with the Confederates led to her association with Quantrell's Raiders and Cole Younger, a one time lover of hers, as well as Frank and Jessie James. On one famous occasion, she rode her horse non-stop 35 miles to warn her brother, who rode with Quantrell, that the Union Army was on its way to get him. She got there before they did, even though she was delayed from leaving at the same time. Unfortunately, even though her frantic ride had saved him, her brother was killed a few days later in another skirmish while riding with Quantrell. She carried a lifetime grudge against any "Yankee" because of that.

When Belle was 20 years old, she married the son of a wealthy farmer. Belle had already met the Youngers and the James boys through her brother and her new husband became friends with them as well. Even though Belle and her husband had both been born into wealthy families, they both had a wild side to them. Her father had been opposed to their wedding, but they ran away together and got married. Her father tried to steal his daughter away from her new husband and send her away for awhile, but they ended up back together in spite of all of his tries to interfere. In September, 1869, Belle gave birth to a daughter. One year after her daughter was born, her husband became a fugitive after killing a man who had killed his brother. As a fugitive, he and Belle and their daughter lived for a while in Los Angeles, California. In 1871, while in California, they had a baby boy. Belle's father had since moved to Dallas, Texas and she and her husband bought a ranch there. It was there that Belle began to build a reputation for owning fine horses.

She had been one of the first in the area to buy "thoroughbreds," which were a cross-breed of Arabian stallions and English mares. They were the fastest and hardiest horses in the country. Belle had always loved fast horses and fast horses were becoming a big business for her. Her husband would stay on the run and would only be able to visit her on occasions. He usually stayed with Tom Starr in the Indian Territory. Starr was a Cherokee and had become known as the "worst Indian" the Cherokee government had ever had to deal with. Starr was a Confederate scout during the Civil War. Tom Starr had a son named Sam Starr, who was younger than Belle and she would end up marrying Sam later on.

In 1873 a Creek Indian was robbed of $30,000 by Belle's husband and others. In 1875, when one of the robbers was being executed, he named Belle's husband as one of the other men who was involved in the robbery. Thereafter, a huge reward was placed on Belle's husband and one of his companions killed him for the reward. When Belle was asked to identify the body of her husband, she said that they had killed the wrong man. She was determined they would not get the reward. The money had been stolen from the Creek Nation in the first place.

Belle had surrounded herself with outlaws but had not been a real outlaw herself until she was scouting with Blue Duck, a notorious Indian outlaw, while a widow. Blue Duck had borrowed $2,000 from Belle and had lost it in a card game. Belle promptly entered the saloon, pulled her pistol and took $7,000 from the men and failed to give them back the change. For some reason, they never pressed charges against her.

In 1880 Belle married Sam Starr. While keeping her spread and horses near Dallas, Belle bought 1,000 acres in a bend in the Canadian River, she named Younger's Bend. The ranch was about 16 miles south of Eufaula and about 30 miles south of Muskogee and about 68 miles southwest of Fort Smith. Her home was always a welcome place for her former husband's friends and outlaws such as Jesse James and Cole Younger who were known to stay there from time to time.

Belle's daughter loved horses and wild rides into the countryside, much like her mother when she was a teenager. She was about 15 when a neighbor became irritated at her wild rides through his ranch and made it a point to kill her fine horse. To make matters worse, a former deputy marshal stole one of the neighbor's best horses and the neighbor charged that Belle and Sam Starr had stolen his horse as retribution for him killing theirs, and had them sent to prison in Detroit for a year. If Bass Reeves had not testified on their behalf, they could have been in prison for a much longer time.

Bass Reeves had testified that the former marshal, not the Starrs, had stolen the horse. Belle Starr was his friend for life after that. Anytime he was near her farm, he would stop by. She would even give him "leads" on outlaws that she knew to be in the area when he was there. He knew that outlaws stayed there from time to time, but he could not help liking Belle. She spoke and acted like a refined woman and reminded him of Colonel Reeves' wife, who was always nice to him and his mother.

Bass continued thinking about his friendship with Belle and her take on life as he rode up the trail to the main ranch house in the Creek Indina Nation. It was an amazing structure, with hand-cut logs fitted together so closely they needed no filling. It was about twice the size of the house Bass built on Mount Vista and had a roof topped with wood cedar shingles. He thought it was beautiful. It sat on top of a hill and overlooked the Canadian River. The view was breathtaking and the pastures that held her best horses were fenced with crossed cedar poles.

Belle came out of her house with a big smile and hugged the big man after he dismounted his horse.

"Bass, you big hunk of a man, what're you doing over here? I heard you killed a bunch of outlaws who tried to go to your house!" she exclaimed.

"That's true, Miz Belle," Bass allowed, "and that's kind of why I'm coming to see you."

"How's that?" Belle asked.

"Well," Bass said, as Belle invited him to come into the house, "I gave marshals some of my horses in appreciation for their help killing those men and protecting my family, and I'm short of good horses to ride."

"Bass," Belle said, "my best horses are still in Texas. Do you want to ride down there with me and pick some out?"

"That'd take a week or longer," Bass said, "why don't we take the train from Eufaula and pick out the horses and then bring them back by train. That'd save us a lot of time."

"Sam will be back tomorrow," Belle said, "can you stay over tonight and go get the horses tomorrow? I don't want to leave my daughter here by herself."

"Sure," Bass replied, "that won't be a problem. I want to buy 5 or 6 of your best horses. How much would you charge me for 'em"

"Well," Belle said "my very best horses are thoroughbreds I had shipped to Texas from overseas. I usually get $300 each for them."

"Oh," Bass said, disappointed, "I only brought $1,000 in gold and silver coins. I didn't think they'd be that high."

"Well," Belle continued, "if you don't get you some of my horses, you're not going to ever be able to catch Jesse James, because he's riding one of my best horses!"

"I thought Jesse was killed three years ago by one of his own men." Bass said

"If that's true, his ghost was just here four days ago," Belle said, "and his ghost stayed here for two days and ate my cooking."

"I'll be damned," Bass uttered, "nobody ever collected the reward, which was $5,000, and that's probably why. I wonder if the reward would still stand if I brought him in or killed him?"

"I don't know," Belle said, "but I'm not going to tell you which direction he went. He is laying low and I probably will never see him again. Sam doesn't like him to stay here when he's gone, but I couldn't turn him down."

"If I could catch him, I could buy a bunch of your horses" Bass allowed.

"Well," Belle said, "I'm not going to wait around here until you catch Jesse James before you go to Dallas and get your horses. If you killed Jesse, the price of the horses would go up… I tell you what, Bass, I'll sell you 5 of my best horses for $200 each, if we can leave tomorrow after Sam gets back."

"That'll save me $500," Bass said, "$500 in the hand is worth $5,000 I might get, so you've got a deal, Belle." He was afraid she'd change her mind if he didn't agree real soon.

"Not only that," Belle said, "but I'll be saving your life as well. I can outdraw you and Jesse can outdraw me." she stated.

Bass knew she was right about her outdrawing him, but he'd have to take her word about Jesse James. If he ever ran into James, he'd try to take him at a distance, where speed of the draw wouldn't matter. That was good to know.

"You know I could shoot him at 300 yards without worrying about how fast he can draw." Bass said.

"I'll admit you're the best in the west when it comes to a rifle," she said, "that's probably how you survived the Civil War. You must've been the only negro fighting for the Confederacy. But that's good, because you know I hate Yankees."

"Believe it or not," Bass replied, "a number of Confederate officers had slaves with them who carried guns and when the shooting started, everybody with guns fired back. We were just defending our lives. We didn't know much about why the war was started. Colonel Reeves always said that the Civil War was about taxes, not about slavery. When southerners refused to pay taxes on their slaves, Lincoln got back at them with the Emancipation Proclamation. At least that's what Colonel Reeves said, but us negros were just hoping to get freedom out of it.

I'll never forget what happened at the Battle of Pea Ridge."

"Weren't you with McCullock's 11th Texas?" Belle asked.

She had heard a lot of horrible stories about some of the battles, but she still had a morbid curiosity about them.

"Yep," Bass replied, "my owner, Colonel George Reeves, was in the 11th Texas Cavalry. I was 21 years old at that time, but I could shoot and ride with anyone. We had about 16,000 troops all together, including about 800 Indians.

The Union General had moved about 10,000 Union Army men and 50 cannons into Arkansas and had set up a position on a hill overlooking Sugar Creek in Benton County, near the Elkhorn Tavern.

Our General wanted us to go around to the backside of the Union troops and cut off their supply lines. We only took 3 days' rations and ammunition and left our supply line behind. We got into a fierce battle at Foster's Farm and they pounded us with cannons. Eventually, when our General realized we had lost our supply line, because someone gave the wrong order, he decided to retreat. We were north of the Union positions and had to go back through the Union lines to get back to our supplies. I saw many men die that day and it was the worst experience I ever had. Compared to that battle, what I do for a living today is easy.

Our Colonel got killed by a Union sniper in the very first battle and nobody took command for him, so it was very confusing for us. There were too many officers who wouldn't follow orders. It was a nightmare."

"I heard that Wild Bill Hickok was a scout for the Union Army in that battle." Belle stated.

"That's what I heard," Bass answered, "but the only Union Army soldiers I saw up close were already dead or dying. I didn't see Hickok."

"I still hate Yankees!" Belle said, "except for Judge Parker. I have a soft spot in my heart for him."

Judge Parker had given her and Sam Starr a lenient sentence of just one year for horse theft after the jury trial. He had believed Bass's testimony, but the jury had not.

Belle fixed Bass a big pan fried steak for dinner, along with potatoes and gravy. She had asked Jesse to kill a calf they'd been feeding when he was there. Bass marveled to Belle about how good her cooking was, as he mopped up the gravy in his plate with one of her delicious oven baked rolls. He could still smell the yeast from the rolls sitting out to rise from the day before.

The inside of Belle's house was really nice, with deer and buffalo horns on the walls. There were also photographs or paintings of all of Belle's famous outlaw friends. Jesse and Frank James, the Younger brothers, Blue Duck and other notable outlaws.

After dinner, they sat out on her back porch, in rocking chairs. Bass dug out his detective pipe and fired it up. Belle's daughter came riding up on her horse and waved to Bass. After she corralled the horse, Belle fed her dinner and she joined them on the porch, as they watched the sun paint the clouds as it sank in the west.

The next day, after Sam got home, Belle and Bass saddled their horses and headed to Eufaula. After boarding their horses at the stables, they boarded the Missouri, Kansas and Texas Rail Road train to Dallas. It was a two-day trip, but much better than riding that distance. It was hard to sleep on a horse and they had to be rested overnight. It would have probably taken them close to a week to get there by horseback and they might've run into horse thieves on the way back. When they arrived in Dallas, they rented a buckboard to take them to the ranch. As they were getting close to the ranch house, Bass started looking at some of the horses he saw out in the pastures and watched how fast they could run. He was impressed by their speed and their size.

"So Belle," Bass asked, "you've been getting $300 apiece for your horses?"

"That's right," Belle said, "at first I just sold a few to outlaws. Then the Texas lawmen had to buy horses from me so they could catch the outlaws."

"That's funny," Bass said, "even to a lawman."

Belle had a sense of humor that really tickled Bass. He wasn't used to a woman being as forward and outrageous as Belle, but that was what made her so much fun.

When they arrived at the ranch house, he wanted to go out and look at the horses. He was excited to be getting a good deal. He planned to buy a couple of stallions and three mares. He would start reproducing some of these thoroughbreds on his own ranch. Soon, the marshals would all want horses as fast as the ones he rode. What he really liked about these horses was the size. Since they were part Arabians, they were big horses that also happened to be fast. He needed big horses because of his size. Small horses didn't last him very long.

He and Belle saddled a couple of horses and rode out into the pastures, along with an Indian who worked for her. Bass finally selected 5 horses that he liked and the Indian proceeded to round them up one by one. By the end of the day he had them in one small fenced area, ready to go. They decided to stay at the ranch overnight and head back to Indian Territory in the morning by train.

The next day, when he and Belle got to the train station, the horses were loaded into a car designed for livestock. Soon, they were on their way back to Eufaula. They awoke the next morning when the train stopped in Durant to get fuel and water and to offload passengers. After a short stop the train was back on its way. They had just left Durant and had not reached full speed, when the train slowed down and stopped again. Bass stuck his head out the window to see what was happening and saw a couple of wagons blocking the track and about a dozen outlaws with their guns drawn and pointed at the engineer, Benjamin Westphal, a man that Bass knew. Benjamin's brother had been killed in another train robbery, so this train wasn't going anywhere. Benjamin wasn't ready to join his brother yet.

"What's going on?" Belle asked.

"You won't believe this," Bass said "but the train is being robbed."

"Well," Belle said, "don't try to be a hero and get yourself killed. If you'll let me go talk to them, I can make sure they don't take the horses."

"Alright," Bass said, "I'll give you time to talk to them. I don't have my rifle, and I'd hate to take on 12 outlaws with two 6 guns." It was everything he could do to keep his seat. He couldn't believe that Belle was going to go talk to the outlaws. She might not know them and get herself killed. If they killed her, he was going to take down as many of them as possible.

Bass didn't intend to allow them to take his horses. He knew if the outlaws didn't find what they were looking for on the train, they'd rob the passengers, but that'd be their last resort. Most of the passengers had sidearms. Most would mind their own business unless they were about to be robbed. There were probably a few railroad detectives on the train somewhere. But they wouldn't try to take on 12 outlaws.

Belle got up and headed to the front of the train, even though she was warned by the conductor not to go up there. As she poked her head out of the first car and looked into the locomotive, guns were pointed at her, seeing that she wore a Colt on her belt.

"Howdy boys," Belle began, "my name is Belle Starr and I recognize a few of you. Jesse James, tell these boys not to be pointing their guns at me."

The order was given to lower their guns.

Belle continued, "Boys, U.S. Marshal Bass Reeves is on this train and it was everything I could do to keep him from coming up here to kill all of you. And you know he could. He can outdraw me or you, Jesse. And he has his rifle with him. He could kill half of you as you ride away. He could hit you out to 500 yards. I've seen him do it."

"What do you want, Belle?" Jesse asked her.

"Well, Jesse," Belle began, "there are 5 of my best horses in that second livestock car and they've been purchased by Bass Reeves for his own personal use. If you boys will stay out of the passenger cars and leave those horses alone and not shoot my friend Benjamin Westphal standing here, I promise to keep Bass from killing you."

One of the men hollered "I would like to see that stinking marshal try to take us all on. We could kill him easy."

"You'd better do as Belle says," Jesse said, "if you piss her off, she might be on his side and help him kill us. She can outdraw me for sure." All of the outlaws knew that Jesse could outdraw them all, so they backed off.

"Belle," Jesse said, "we are after a $100,000 shipment from the U.S. Government to the Indian Territory capitol of Tishomingo." That's all we plan to take. It's in a car at the rear of the train, in front of the caboose. I'm gonna' take some men around the train to get to the safe and blow it with dynamite. If you keep Reeves in his seat, we'll leave after we get the money. This'll be my last job, and I hope I'm still a welcome guest at your place."

"You know you're always welcome at my place," Belle said, winking at Jesse.

"I may see you soon." Jesse countered."

"We have a deal!" Belle said and then turned and went back to Bass.

When she got back to him, she could tell he was wanting to get into a gunfight in the worst way, but after she told him she'd made a deal to leave the passengers alone and his horses alone, he agreed to stay put.

The outlaws went to the rear of the train. Bass and Belle could hear the explosion and feel the impact as it rocked all of the cars on the train. It felt like the train had hit a boulder or something. The cars rocked back and forth for a few seconds. Bass had to stick his head out of the car, even though the conductor had come through all of the cars and warned the passengers to keep their heads inside. He could see the outlaws picking up money off the ground and stuffing it in their saddlebags.

After they had picked up all the money the outlaws rode away and the train resumed the trip to Eufaula and on to Muskogee. When they got to Eufaula, the conductor sent wires to Muskogee and Fort Smith, telling them what had happened. Bass figured he'd probably be coming back this way with warrants, once they figured out who the outlaws were. He'd try to get Belle to identify them, if possible. She must have gotten a good look at them.

"Belle," he asked, "who were the outlaws you made the deal with?"

"Bass," she said, "the only one of them that I knew for sure was Jesse James and you know nobody is going to believe you if you say it was him, because he's supposed to be dead. They all had masks on, but I knew it was Jesse. Two of them were colored and three of them were Indian. I think one of them used to ride with Quantrell. He may be a Dalton."

Bass was tired after they got off the train at Eufaula and agreed to spend the night again at Belle's. The next morning he was ready to get his new horses and hit the trail back to Mount Vista. Bass began to wonder if Judge Parker would be upset that he didn't try to stop the train robbery.

On he got back to Fort Smith, Bass checked in with Judge Parker. Parker was not upset that Bass didn't engage the outlaws.

The judge said, "That many men would be hard for even you to tangle, especially without your rifle. Keeping those outlaws from robbing the passengers and possibly killing one or more of them was more important than trying to shoot some of them. The U.S. Government will just send another $100,000 to the Indians, but I wouldn't be surprised if the Army didn't make it their business to chase those outlaws down. That would save us the trouble."

"That's true," Bass replied, "but a couple of those men already have rewards on them, and you know the Missouri, Kansas and Texas Rail Road will put rewards on everyone who robbed the train. So I wouldn't mind trying to run them down myself."

"Did Belle recognize any of the outlaws?" Judge Parker asked.

"Well, you won't believe this," Bass answered, "but Belle said one of them was Jesse James and another was someone who had ridden with Quantrell, maybe a Dalton ."

"That doesn't surprise me," Judge Parker said, "I thought there was something fishy about Jesse James' death."

"Is there still a reward on him?" Bass asked.

"There's still a $5,000 reward on him by the railroad," Judge Parker said. "You would have to get Belle to identify him. And I bet there is at least a $5,000 reward on any of the Daltons. At one time they were worth $10,000 each."

"Well," Bass said, "If you'd give me warrants on James and Dalton. I'd be just about ready to go see if I could catch them."

"I'll do that tomorrow," Judge Parker said, "but I have a favor to ask of you before you go out chasing outlaws again."

"What's that?" Bass answered.

"We're going to put on a wild west show here in Fort Smith in about a week to commemorate the anniversary of the court and I would like Belle Starr to pretend to rob a stagecoach. I'll be one of the passengers and I want her to rob me at gunpoint. I think that would be a lot of fun and people would come all the way from Little Rock and Siloam Springs to see something like this. We might even get some people to come down from Missouri, where Belle is from. And maybe even from Texas!"

"That would be a lot of fun, Judge," Bass allowed, "I know my family would enjoy that. I'll ride back over there and ask her. It will be my first chance to ride one of my new horses."

He was anxious to ride a grey thoroughbred stallion he had brought back. It was really spirited. He liked the look in its eye. Grey thoroughbreds were fairly rare and he had only seen one other.

The next day, after getting his five new horses pastured, he saddled the grey that he now called "Lightning" and headed back to Belle's ranch. Maybe, if he got lucky, he'd catch Jesse James there. He didn't think Belle would take sides if that happened. He made sure to take his trusty Winchester .38-.40 and filled up a pocket on his saddlebags with cartridges, just to be sure he had enough ammo if he did get into a gunfight. It was a two-day trip, but he decided not to take a wagon or a posse man with him and would camp out on the way there. The weather was good, so he didn't bother with a tent. He packed enough food to eat in his saddlebags.

Riding up to Belle's house on the second day, Bass kept a sharp eye out for extra horses or any other indication that Jesse might be there, but he didn't see anything that looked unusual. He still kept one hand ready to grab a pistol as he rode up to the house.

As usual, Belle had heard him coming and greeted him from the front porch. "If you're here looking for Jesse James," she said, "you're a day late. And he still has that wild bunch with him. The other one that I recognized was Bob Dalton. I hadn't seen him since the Northfield robbery. If you're going after them, you'd better get yourself a posse man or two. Or some more marshals."

Bass couldn't help but chuckle to himself. No woman in her right mind would put up twelve outlaws of that sort. They were just as apt to rape as to steal, but Belle had no fear. At least no fear that he could see. "I didn't come here to find Jesse and his gang," Bass replied, "I came to ask you a favor for Judge Parker."

"How is that cantankerous old fart?" Belle asked, in her usual outrageous manner.

"He's doing pretty good and its a good thing he didn't hear you say that about him, or you might end up in his jail instead of a wild west show." Bass said.

"What wild west show?" Belle asked.

"Judge Parker is planning a big wild west show on the next anniversary of his court which is next week. He seems to be more excited about that than hanging outlaws." Bass answered. "He wants you to pretend to rob a stagecoach he's on and rob him."

"It would be mighty tempting to just take the old fart's money for real," Belle said, laughing, "but seriously you know I owe the judge a favor. I'd be thrilled to take part in the show. Count me in!"

"As soon as you hold up the stage and rob the judge," Bass said, "I'll be there to chase you out of town. We'll get to see if this grey horse you sold me is as fast as you say it is."

"He's pretty fast," Belle said, "but I'll be riding a red thoroughbred mare that may give him a good race. Tell you what, I'll bet you $200 that you can't catch me before dark sets in."

"That's a bet," Bass said, "be sure and bring the money with you."

"You'd better bring money with you," Belle said playfully, "you'll need it. Get down off that horse and come on in. I have a steak I can warm up for you, if you don't mind eatin' outlaw's leftovers."

That made Bass laugh out so hard, it startled his horse. After getting the horse back under control, he tied it to the hitching post and went inside. One of Belle's Indians then took the horse to the stable for the night.

After a good meal and a good night's sleep, Bass rode back to Fort Smith. He was starting to look forward to this wild west show. He could chase the outlaws later. He knew Belle would probably tell him where they'd gone. They were not likely to leave the Indian Territory and were probably headed to "No Man's Land", about 500 miles from Fort Smith.

7

Buffalo Bill Cody

Judge Parker was as giddy as a child when it was time for the wild west show to begin. He'd arranged to get "Buffalo Bill" Cody to bring his *Buffalo Bill's Wild West Show* to Fort Smith. Cody was thrilled to know that Belle Starr was going to participate.

William Frederick "Buffalo Bill" Cody was born on a farm near LeClaire, Iowa in 1846. When Cody was only 14, he decided to go west and pan for gold, but on his way to California, he met someone with the Pony Express and signed on. He rode for the Pony Express until about 1868 when he became a scout for the U.S. Army at the age of 22. He was Chief of Scouts for the Third Cavalry during the Plains Wars. In 1872, at the age of 26, he received the Medal of Honor for service to the U.S. Army as a scout. It was in 1872 when he traveled to Chicago to make his debut as an "actor." Later, near Platte, Nebraska, he founded *Buffalo Bill's Wild West*. Annie Oakley was a sharpshooter who had joined the show.

As part of the show, Judge Parker rode in a stagecoach through Fort Smith down Garrison Avenue. Belle Starr came chasing after the stagecoach on her red thoroughbred mare to cheers from the crowd. She had several of her Indian employees dressed up as her "gang." She rode to the front of the stagecoach and pointed her Colt at the driver and ordered him to pull over. Then she went to the passenger door and dragged Judge Parker out of the stagecoach and once again, the crowd cheered with glee!

Belle then took Parker's billfold, which had fake money in it and then gave him a big kiss right on his lips. The crown roared! Parker was thrilled and embarrassed at the same time. It was just like Belle to do something that outrageous. The crowd would never forget this part of the show and neither would Judge Isaac Parker.

"That'll give you something to remember me by," Belle said, as she smiled at the look on Judge Parker's face, "just in case you don't see me again."

"I don't think I could ever forget you, Belle!" the Judge replied.

Then, just like they had arrived, the "gang" on cue headed to Indian Territory, just as Bass Reeves arrived to chase them out of town. By the time they entered the Arkansas River to cross into Indian Territory, Bass had already caught the "gang" and dispatched them with fake gunfire. The grey thoroughbred that Bass had bought from Belle had no problem catching the ordinary horses the "gang" rode. Catching the red thoroughbred that Belle was riding would not be as easy. She looked like she was pulling away from him already.

Bass chased Belle for about 20 miles before she was finally gone from his sight. He finally decided to turn back to Fort Smith, since this was only a game, but he decided he would try to buy that red mare the next time he saw Belle Starr. In the meantime he owed her $200. She wouldn't let him forget that, or the fact she had beaten him. Nothing surprised him about Belle. He laughed out loud, thinking about her kissing Judge Parker.

The wild west show was still going on when Bass rode back into town well before dark. Annie Oakley was throwing whiskey glasses into the air and shooting them with her .45. When Bass rode up, several people in the crowd urged him to shoot some glasses and see if he was better than Oakley. She had shot 10 glasses in a row before missing one. Bass took out his guns and shot 12 in a row, with 12 shots.

Irritated that she had been beaten with a pistol, Oakley challenged him to a long distance shooting contest with a rifle and he accepted. She walked off 500 yards and set a target up in the sand. She then walked back up to Bass and let him have the first shot. He promptly put a .38-40 cartridge into the chamber of his Winchester rifle and shooting without the aid of a rest, placed a hole in the dead center of the target. Oakley's shot was 3 inches low and right of dead center.

She screamed with anger and walked away. "I'm going to the saloon to get a drink!" she shouted. The crowd cheered Bass to the point where he was embarrassed. The crowd urged him to go to the saloon for a drink, but Bass declined. He did not drink. But, he decided to stay overnight in Fort Smith, because it was getting dark.

The grand finale of the show was a staged Indian attack on a settler's cabin. Cody rode in with a group of cowboys to defend the settler and his family. This was the first time Cody had used this act in his show. Judge Parker was offended by this portrayal of Indians and told Cody so. Cody said he would continue to use this as part of his show anyway and he continued to use it in his show 23 more times before stopping in 1907.

Judge Parker had always been impressed by the honesty of the Indians he had met. They would never lie in court, even to protect themselves. He never even made Indians put up bail money. If they promised to show up, they would, even when they were charged with murder. Because of the indian portrayal, he never asked Cody to do another show in Fort Smith. It was Parker's job to protect the Indians from mostly white outlaws and he would never intentionally insult them. The judge was thankful there weren't many Indians in the crowd.

The next morning, on his way back to Mount Vista, Bass began to plan his trip to No Man's Land. He would begin his trip by going to see Belle Starr again. She would tell him for sure if that was where Jesse James, Bob Dalton and their gang were headed. He would take her the $200 he owed her and another $400 to see if she would sell the red thoroughbred. He would probably need at least 3 more marshals to take on that many men, especially considering the gunfighting skills of James and Dalton.

Once he had rested and decided which horses to ride, he'd return to Fort Smith to see which marshals wanted to go with him and to gather his wagons and supplies. Judge Parker had promised to have warrants ready for the outlaws by the time Bass was ready to leave. In the meantime, the Missouri, Kansas and Texas Rail Road had extended rewards for Jesse James and Bob Dalton at $10,000 each, as a result of their reported robbery of the train carrying $100,000 to the Indian Nation.

They had also offered a reward of $5,000 each for any gang members riding with them. This would be a very rewarding trip and Bass was sure that he wouldn't have any trouble getting other marshals to ride with him. The U.S. Army said they would prefer that U.S. Marshals go after the outlaws, since the Indian Territory was their jurisdiction. Besides, Judge Parker had asked that his marshals be the ones who brought the outlaws to justice. And the army respected his wishes.

The next morning, Bass saddled the grey thoroughbred, Lightning, and decided to take Silver on the trip for luck. He put a bridle on Silver and proceeded to ride down the mountain and cross the river into Fort Smith. His first priority was to go see Judge Parker and get the warrants.

"Morning Judge," Bass said, "do you have those warrants ready for me?"

"Bass," Judge Parker said, "I have warrants for Jesse James and Bob Dalton for train robbery and I have warrants for any of the other gang members you can catch or kill. J. H. Merchon is out serving warrants already, but William P. Pittcock, Bud Kell and Heck Thomas have all said they'd go with you. They are in Marshal Boles' office. Rumor has it, the outlaws were headed for No Man's Land. You will probably encounter Chocktaw, Creek, Seminole and Cherokee Indians, among others, on your trip, so your ability to speak their languages will come in handy. I don't think the Indians will bother you.

They know the train robbers took money that was rightfully theirs, so they should be on your side. If the Lighthorse had any jurisdiction over white men, they probably would've taken them on. I bet they'll know where they are if they went through Indian Territory. No Man's Land is close to 500 miles from Fort Smith, so it will probably take you at least 2 weeks to get there. When you get there, you may encounter other gangs in that area. If you do, go ahead and kill or capture anyone who gets in your way. The warrants I gave you will allow you to do that."

"Yessir, Judge." Bass said.

When he walked into Marshal Boles' office, he found Pittcock, Kell and Thomas waiting for him.

"Men," Bass began, "I thank all of you for agreeing to come with me on this trip. We're going to be traveling for at least two weeks before we get to No Man's Land, which is where we think they're headed. We'll be going up against gunmen who won't think twice about killing any of us."

"The risk of getting shot is high. The rewards are also high. We stand to collect as much as $70,000 if we manage to kill or capture the gang. Or we might just get a few of them and only get $5,000 or so. We'll equally split whatever we get. Judge Parker said he'll pay for our travel and our normal fees. Do you have any questions?"

"I've heard Jesse James is very fast with a pistol," Heck Thomas stated, "have you heard the same?"

"Belle Starr said Jesse could outdraw her," Bass answered, "although she lied about that during the train robbery... and she can outdraw me."

"That's pretty fast," Heck said, "I think you're probably faster than all of us."

"I don't know about that," Pittcock interjected, "I think I can take Bass."

Everyone in the room laughed at that, including Boles, who was almost as fast as Bass.

"Let's go get our supplies and take them to the wagon," Bass said, "we're going to need a lot of ammunition. We probably need to get some dynamite in case they're holed up in a cave. I have the cook wagon loaded with food. I've brought along an extra horse and I see you have also. I see you have some of my horses. I brought Silver along so he could see his old friends."

The horses acted like they were familiar with each other. Sometimes horses didn't get along and it wasn't unusual for horses to fight with each other, even with their riders on them, especially stallions. So it was good to have a little more harmony among the horses.

It would be a very long trip, so they brought tents to sleep in. They wouldn't be picking up any prisoners along the way, like they normally would, because they'd need all of the room in the prison wagon to haul the gang back, alive or dead. They could tie the outlaw's horses to the prison wagon or the cook's wagon. Bass had specified that he wanted Jesse James' horse if they managed to catch him. Belle, like Bass, didn't believe in branding horses, but Bass thought he'd recognize any horses that'd belonged to Belle. They'd stand out in a group of ordinary horses.

When the 4 marshals rode down Garrison Avenue trailing a horse each and accompanied by a cook wagon and a prison wagon, the people walking down the street knew that something big was happening. Bart Simms, owner of the *Fort Smith Weekly Elevator,* hurried over to Marshal Boles office to see if he could get the scoop on what was happening. He was breathless by the time he got to the marshal's office.

"Marshal Boles," he began, "can you tell me what's going on? Why are all of those marshals headed out of town? Who are they going after?"

"They're going after Jesse James," Marshal Boles replied, "we think he's still alive and hiding out in Indian Territory."

"Jesse James was killed by his own man," Bart argued, "everybody knows that."

"His death was faked," Marshal Boles said, "and the reward was never collected. Marshal Reeves saw him rob a train about two weeks ago."

"What did the robbers get?" Simms asked.

"They got $100,000 that was from the U.S. Government and was going to the Indian Nation." Boles said.

"Wow!" Simms said. "I'd heard about that, but didn't know for sure. Who else was with Jesse James?"

"We think Bob Dalton was also with him." Boles said.

"Wow!" Simms said again. "This'll be quite a scoop. Thanks Marshal Boles!"

"Just make sure you get your facts straight this time." Boles warned.

"Oh I will." Simms said.

Regardless of whether that was true or not, Bart Simms knew he had one hell of a story and he was going to print it, truth or not. The next day, the paper's front page blared the headlines:

JESSE JAMES ALIVE AND SEEN BY MARSHAL

It seems that Marshal Bass Reeves witnessed a train robbery a few weeks back, where he was too cowardly to take on the robbers by himself, and says he spotted Jesse James himself leading a bunch of desperados, including Bob Dalton, who stole $100,000 in Indian money from the train. Marshal Reeves was so scared of the great Jesse James, who is said to be the fastest gun in the west, that he hid in the passenger car of the train until the desperados were gone, before making his presence known.

It seems that Marshal Reeves came back to Fort Smith with his tail tucked between his legs to get three other mar-

shals to help him go after them. Even then, he waited until he could act like a hero in the wild west show to gather the courage to ride out after them. Jesse James' previously reported death was obviously faked by his friends, according to Marshal Boles. Judge Parker has issued warrants for their arrest."

Judge Parker was so mad when he read the paper the next day, that he thought about throwing Simms into jail just for the fun of it. But he managed to reason with himself and refrain from doing anything. But he vowed that if Simms ever was arrested for almost anything, he would do jail time.

Bass Reeves' wife, Jennie was in town getting groceries, when she saw the article. She was angry about the article as well and saved it for Bass to read. That guy is stupid, she thought to herself. Bass will do something about this.

Billy Washington was so excited about the article that he gave Simms another $500. Simms was excited about the $500. Billy Washington was happy to cause Bass any grief that he could. His association with Billy Simms was beginning to pay off. And he had an idea about how he could make it even worse.

One of Bob Dalton's friends saw the article also. He sent a wire to a mutual friend of theirs, near No Man's Land, to warn him that Reeves was coming, along with 3 other marshals. He knew that Dalton was with James. So the outlaws would know who was coming after them and would have a pretty good idea when they would get there.

They had holed up in a log structure that had been a temporary fort at one time, sitting up on a hill that overlooked most of the surrounding land. They could see for miles and anyone approaching would have little cover to hide behind. They would be ready. There were 12 of them against 4 marshals. They weren't worried.

As many outlaws as there were hiding out in No Man's Land, the marshals might get killed before they even got there. The hideout was in the foothills of Black Mesa, the highest elevation in Oklahoma. And the marshals would have to cross the Cimarron River from the South, while in rifle range. They wouldn't stand a chance. Black Mesa was about 180 miles past the border of No Man's Land. That would put them about 680 miles from Fort Smith. Just to make things interesting, Jesse posted reward posters throughout No Man's Land offering $1,000 each for any of the marshals who were captured or killed on their way through.

"Let's see how the marshals like having a price on their head." Jesse said to Bob Dalton, as they hammered the posters to trees along the trails. They both had a good laugh about that.

8

The Pursuit of Jesse James and Bob Dalton

Two days had passed before the marshals reached Belle Starr's ranch on the Canadian River. They'd eaten enough beans and biscuits to be looking forward to Belle's home cooking. As they rode up to the ranch house, they saw Belle riding up from the west. She had been out in the pasture and saw them coming up the road.

"That's a good looking white horse you're leading, Bass, did you bring him to me to settle your debt?" Belle teasingly greeted the marshal, "How're the rest of you gentlemen?"

"We're doing well Ma'am," the other 3 marshals chimed in, "How're you doing?"

"Well," Belle said, "I'm always happy to see a bunch of good looking men come ridin' up. Especially when one of them owes me money."

"Belle," Bass said, a little bit embarrassed, "I brought you that $200 that I owe you on that bet. I see you're riding that horse that won it for you. I will give you another $300 for that horse."

"Really?" Belle asked, "how about $400?"

"You have a deal," Bass said, "but you'll have to keep her until I get back from No Man's Land. I don't expect to have to chase anybody once we get there."

"You'll have to call her Ruby," Belle said, laughing at the idea of him riding a Ruby.

"You're kidding me!" Bass said, "I can't be riding no horse named Ruby!"

"Well," Belle said, "you can't have her if you want to change her name. That'll make her unhappy."

"I'll have to think about that," Bass said, "can I give you my answer when I get back? I'll let you hold the money until then."

"That's a deal," Belle said, "you may get killed and I'll get to keep the money and the horse," she teased, "you boys hungry?" They all shook their heads together. "It'll take me a little time," Belle said, "but I'll fix you boys some of the best steaks you've ever eaten."

"That sounds great," Bass said, "she's telling the truth, she cooks a mean steak."

Belle handed Ruby over to her Indian hand and told the marshals to tie their horses up and the Indian would take care of them later. The marshals followed her to the house and followed her orders to go set on the porch until she'd finished cooking dinner. Her back porch had plenty of rocking chairs, so they just sat rocking, watching the sun as it set over the Canadian River. There were some clouds in the sky and they were painted a bright orange color by the setting sun. There were a bunch of crows bickering out in the pasture and Belle's fine horses were grazing peacefully.

The quiet didn't last long, because Heck Thomas just had to say something about Bass losing a bet to Belle. In spite of his rough look, Heck was known to have a sense of humor.

"How come you owe Belle $200?" Heck asked.

"Do you remember when I chased her out of town after that stagecoach robbery when she kissed Judge Parker? She'd bet me that I couldn't catch her by dark. That red horse of hers flat outran the grey horse I'm riding, that she sold me for $200."

Heck continued to pick at Bass, "So now you're going to be riding a horse named Ruby, just so you can outrun everybody? All you'd have to do when you got after somebody would be to shout out 'my horse is named Ruby' real loud and the outlaw would laugh so hard he'd fall off his horse!" All of the marshals had a good laugh about that. It was hard to imagine Bass riding a horse named Ruby. Every time they thought about that, they'd start laughing again.

"Allright," Bass said, "you can all laugh at me now, but I'll be catching all of the outlaws and getting all the rewards."

"But is it worth your self respect?" Heck asked, laughing out loud again. "What's next, are you going to name your rifle Winny?" Again they all laughed.

"What're you boys laughing so hard about?" Belle said, as she brought them a glass of tea.

"We're laughing about Marshal Bass Reeves riding his horse Ruby and shooting bad guys with his rifle named Winny." Heck answered.

Belle laughed harder than the men at that thought. She was happy to have started the men teasing Bass. She enjoyed being outrageous. Marshals weren't such hard men that she couldn't have fun with them. She could get along with them and still get along with some of her outlaw friends. "I'm afraid Bass would try to kill all of you if you started talking like that around town. That would give that newspaper editor, Bart Simms something to talk about."

"If I killed anybody," Bass said, "it would be that twerp. He is beholden to Billy Washington and Washington would like nothing better than to cause me problems."

"Well, men," Belle said, "now that I've interrupted the fun you were having, I think I'll go back and finish dinner."

"Bass," Pittcock asked, "is Billy Washington still trying to harm your family?"

"I don't think so," Bass said, "I think Judge Parker scared the hell out of him at his arraignment and he still has to go to trial over that. I just think he'll try to make trouble for me in any way that he can. I heard that Bart Simms had financial troubles and that Washington and McLish bailed him out. I think they pay him anytime he can find something to print about me that's bad."

"We need to run that little twerp out of town," Bud Kell said. "That newspaper is an embarrassment to Fort Smith. I think he just makes up half the stuff you see in there."

"Maybe I will buy the newspaper," Pittcock said, "I've always wanted to be a journalist."

"If you could spell," Heck said, "that might not be a bad idea. And, you would have to be able to read!" Everybody laughed at Pittcock about that. They knew he could barely read and couldn't spell worth a darn.

Pretty soon, Belle came and got them and they all sat down to dinner. Bass asked if he could say grace and Belle said that was alright with her.

"Dear Lord," he began, "please bless this meal and the nice lady who fixed it and please keep all these men safe as we go into No Man's Land to bring to justice these evil men that we're after. Amen."

The steaks were cooked to perfection and the mashed potatoes and gravy were wonderful as well. And Belle had made her famous rolls. And again, you could still smell the yeast where they'd been setting to "rise" before she cooked them. That smell had made them all instantly hungry.

"Ms. Belle," Heck Thomas allowed, "this is the best food I've had in my mouth in ages! I had no idea how good you could cook! No wonder Bass keeps coming over this way every time he's on a trip. I was beginning to think there was something goin' on between you two."

"Oh, Heck!" Belle said, "you're such a cutup! You know that Bass and I are just friends! My husband would scalp him if he thought there was anything between us."

"Well I'll tell you one thing," Heck said, "the next time I'm anywhere near here, I plan on coming by here if you'll allow it! I'd even be willing to cut some firewood or do other work for one of your meals."

"Heck," Belle said, "you can just do like Bass does. He always brings me flour or salt or sugar or other things I can't get around here. I have cattle here for meat and I have a smokehouse filled with lamb and pork, and all kinds of eggs, but I don't have those other things."

"That's a deal," Heck said. "It'd be my pleasure to bring those things to you anytime I come by here."

"I'll do that too," Pittcock said.

"And me too," Bud Kell said.

"Well," Belle said, "that means I won't have to go to town nearly as often! I'd rather stay out here on my ranch than to be anywhere else in the world. Besides, it probably wouldn't be a bad idea to have a few more friends who're lawmen. Any time any of you are around here, you're welcome to come by and eat and stay the night. My husband won't mind. When you're here, I can let you know what I might need on your next trip. We can help each other out. But you'll have to promise not to bother any outlaw friends of mine while they're here. You can arrest them some other time."

"That sounds like a reasonable request, Belle," Bass said, "we all appreciate your hospitality. When I last talked to you, you told me that Jesse James was through here with his gang. Do you know for sure where he was headed?"

"Well, I knew you were going to ask me that," Belle said, "and I don't mind telling you, because you'll find out anyway. All of the Lighthorse in Indian Territory are talking about them and where they've been spotted. You know all of the Lighthorse and I'm sure you can find out where they are. Jesse told me they were headed to a hideout at Black Mesa."

"There is an old log army fort on top of a hill that looks down for a long ways. You would have to cross the Cimarron River in rifle range of the fort, unless you went way upriver and crossed and came back down the river. The River runs from the Northwest corner of No Man's Land to the Southwest corner of No Man's Land. You can't just go around it. It'll be hard to get them out of there. You have to travel across about 170 miles of No Man's Land to get there and there won't be anyone you meet who'll be happy to see a lawman. You'd be better off to hide your badges when you get there."

"What would you do to get 'em out of there if you were us." Bass asked.

"I'd probably come at the Fort from the top of Black Mesa if you can find a way to get to the top. You'd have to come in from the North. The fort faces to the South. If you could come at them early in the morning, that might give you an advantage. Those boys like to party and stay up late at night. They don't like gettin' up early. They'll have some Mexican women with 'em. They have plenty of guns and plenty of ammo and plenty of food and whiskey. They may have other outlaws with them. Sometimes they have as many as 20 other outlaws there at one time. Jesse told me the train robbery was going to be his last job and he planned to go to Mexico with his girlfriend after it was safe to travel back across the Indian Territory, but that might be months from now."

"We ain't going to wait that long," Bass said. "We aim to get going that way tomorrow at first light. We were hoping to eat some of your fine biscuits in the morning before leaving."

"I'll fix you boys the finest breakfast you've ever had in the morning." Belle said.

"We're looking forward to that!" Heck said.

"You boys can all make yourself at home in the bunkhouse," Belle said, "you'll have it all to yourselves."

"Thanks Belle!" they said. "See you in the morning."

The next morning they put their clothes and boots on and went over to the main ranch house, where Belle already had a breakfast of ham and eggs and some small chunks of steak that were left over from the night before. She had also cooked some fine biscuits and gravy. They said very little as they consumed the meal. There were very few leftovers. This was fine food compared to what they'd be eatin' on the trail. Belle gave them a fresh cured ham to take with them on the road. They were very grateful.

This would be the first time any of the marshals had ever entered into No Man's Land. There was no law there, except the 6-shooter or rifle. Mostly it was a hideout for the worst kind of outlaws. Outlaws had little fear of being bothered there, so they might be just a little careless. The marshals knew there was a possibility that word might get to Jesse and his gang prior to their arrival, so they wouldn't plan on surprise being in their favor.

Belle had been there before and she suggested they follow the Canadian River to its fork, just North of her ranch and then follow the North Fork of the Canadian River. When they reached Fort Supply, the last military fort in Indian Territory, they would go Northwest up to the Cimarron River. Belle suggested they then follow the Cimarron River across the Northeast corner of No Man's Land, and then out of No Man's land into Kansas, avoiding most of the travel through No Man's Land. Then she told them to follow the Cimarron River across Kansas and Colorado and then back into No Man's Land just north of Black Mesa. When they got there, they could try to pick a trail to the top of Black Mesa. Belle had drawn them a rough map on a piece of canvas. It would be waterproof when they rolled it up.

This route would skirt No Man's Land to the north. That would avoid travelling through about 150 miles of No Man's Land. They would only have to cross a 20 mile stretch. That way, they wouldn't have to worry about getting into gunfights with outlaws they weren't after. This would also give them the best chance of approaching the hideout undetected. Jesse James would probably be expecting to hear from some of his friends as the marshals crossed No Man's Land.

"We'll be going through Cherokee territory just before we get to No Man's Land," Bass said, as they were getting ready to mount their horses, "I know a Cherokee Indian, who is a Lighthorse policeman and knows No Man's Land like the back of his hand. We should probably hire him to scout for us. If anybody can find a way to get to the top of Black Mesa, he can." The rest of the marshals agreed. All of them dreaded the long trip ahead of them. It was too bad most of the railroads went North and South through Indian Territory and none of them, at that time, went East to West. They would be crossing three different railroads on their way, but none of them were going in the right direction.

It took them 9 days to reach Fort Supply. There, they were able to pick up more supplies of food and other things they would need on the rest of the trip. It was at Fort Supply that Bass met up with John Running Bear, the Lighthorse police with the Cherokee Nation.

"Bass," Running Bear exclaimed, "what're you doing this far from Fort Smith?"

"Running Bear," Bass answered, "these men me are U.S. Marshals Heck Thomas, Bud Kell and William P. Pittcock. We've come all the way over here in pursuit of Jesse James and Bob Dalton and about 10 other men who're riding with 'em. Have you heard about 'em coming through here?"

"All of the Lighthorse across Indian Territory have been talking about those men. They robbed a train carrying $100,000 from the U.S. Government to the Indian capitol in Tishomingo. That robbery has placed a hardship on many Indians. If the Lighthorse had any jurisdiction in the matter, we would've killed these men before they came this far, but as you know, our treaties don't give us that power. The Lighthorse tracked them all the way to Black Mesa. We know they're there and haven't left. There are a few people going back and forth to get supplies. Some Mexican women were brought in shortly after they got to Black Mesa."

"Running Bear," Bass began, "It's our plan to go north from here to the Cimarron River and follow it across the corner of No Man's Land and up into Kansas and then follow it all the way across Kansas and Colorado and then back down into No Man's Land. That way, we can avoid going across most of No Man's Land. We suspect we'd have outlaws shooting at us all the way, if we don't go around it. And we understand the best approach to their hideout would be to come in from the north. What do you think about that?"

"Bass," Running Bear answered, "I think avoiding No Man's Land as much as possible would be the smart thing to do. Once upon a time, when that hideout was an army fort, Blue Goose and some other renegade Indians attacked the fort from the north. They got into the hills above the fort and picked them off one at a time. That's one reason the army abandoned that fort. It has a weakness. I doubt if any of those outlaws know about that. They probably just figure that most people approaching there would be using the old Santa Fe Trail and coming from the south. In that case, anyone approaching the fort would be sitting ducks as they cross the Cimarron River right in front of the fort.

Approaching from the north won't be easy," Running Bear continued, "because you'd have to climb up into the hills. Blue Duck's men walked up the hill, with their horses trailing behind.

Once you get to the top of Black Mesa, you can see a long way in every direction. If friends come to help them, you would be able to pick them off before they got to the fort with a rifle. I've seen you shoot a rifle, Bass and I know you could hit someone all the way to the river from the top of Black Mesa."

"Well, Running Bear," Bass responded, "would you be willing to scout for us and take us to the top of the hill? I know that legally you couldn't do any of the shooting unless we deputize you. Would you be willing to do that?"

"Bass," Running Bear said, "you know you're considered a brother of the Cherokee and speak our native tongue, so it'd make me happy to be with you and help you in any way I can. They have stolen Indian money, and it will be some time before the U.S. Government replaces that money. They've caused hardship for some of our people. I can get more Lighthorse to help if you need that."

"Counting you," Bass said, "there are 5 of us. If we took any more deputies, it wouldn't be a fair fight." All of the marshals had a good laugh at that.

"Yep," Bud Kell said, "if we got too many of us, we might just end up shooting each other. Besides, we're trying to sneak up on them and there's a limit to how many people you can have and still be sneaky." Everybody laughed again. Marshals weren't known to be sneaky.

They decided to stay at Fort Supply until the next morning and leave at daylight. It would take them about 6 days to reach Black Mesa.

The next day they began their trip at first light. They managed to ride from Fort Supply up into Kansas without seeing any other humans except for a few Indians and a few whiskey peddlers. Normally they would've arrested anyone suspected of "introducing" whiskey to the Indians, but they had more important things to do. It was another 5 days to Black Mesa and that travel was made without interruption, other than to stop and camp at nightfall. Following the river not only made navigation easier, but there was always fresh water for them and their horses.

On the 6th day of their trip, they crossed the Cimarron River and headed South to Black Mesa. When they got there, Running Bear told them to dismount and lead one horse each to the top. They tied the remaining four horses at the bottom of the hill. Bass decided to ride Silver to the top, because he didn't want to leave him behind. Besides, Silver would look like a goat way up high, even if the outlaws did spot him. Running Bear took the marshals through a complicated series of trails that led to the top. The only living things they saw were a few wild goats, some lizards and a few rattlesnakes. The goats made the climb to the top look easy, but it was a lot harder for men and horses.

Once the men reached the top of the mesa, they each positioned themselves where they and their horses would be somewhat shielded by boulders. Taking their rifles from their scabbards and their saddle bags holding cartridges with them, they would wait until the next morning. Their plan was to shoot first and ask questions later. If the outlaws were smart, they would run up a white flag to stop the shooting. But most likely the outlaws would try to cross the river on their horses if they decided to run.

The marshals could hear the partying going on at the fort for most of the night. There was music and dancing and whiskey and all kinds of fun going on down there. The marshals were happy just knowing the advantage they would have in the morning. Half of the outlaws would still be drunk.

As daybreak was beginning, Bass told the others "I'm going to throw a stick of dynamite into the compound. That should get them moving. The first outlaw you see, go ahead and shoot him. Try not to kill any of the women if they don't shoot back. We're going to bring them back dead or alive and I don't want to have to bring any of you back shot up or dead, so be careful not to expose yourselves any more than necessary." Bass then threw a stick of dynamite at the compound and it fell a little short, outside the walls of the compound. Lighting another stick, he quickly threw it and it landed on the roof of one of the buildings.

Both sticks went off, almost at the same time. One blew a hole in the back wall and the other blew a hole in the roof of a building. As soon as the first stick of dynamite went off, the outlaws began scrambling around getting clothes on and getting their guns. Soon after, there was wild gunfire towards the marshals.

It was clear they had surprised the outlaws. They were shooting up into the rocks, without even knowing what they were shooting at. Most of the shots didn't even come close to the marshals, but one barely grazed Running Bear. The marshals then killed 6 of the outlaws who were firing at them. As Bass had suspected, 6 men then came riding through and out the front gates of the fort on horses, wildly firing rifles back towards the rocks as they rode.

Two of the riders quickly took the lead by several horse lengths. Bass expected that would be Jesse James and Bob Dalton, riding Belle's thoroughbreds. He concentrated on them and took aim at the first man, about 350 yards away, killing his horse and spilling the rider. He hated that he had killed the horse, even though he was aiming at the rider. The rider was laying on the ground unconscious. He then took aim at the second man out in front, who must have been at least 400 yards away by that time, and killed him without hurting the horse. He felt better about that shot.

The other marshals killed the other 4 men before they could reach the river. Running Bear made the comment "Now you know why the U.S. Army abandoned this fort. It could not be defended from the rear, even though Black Mesa was the highest point in Indian Territory. You would think they would have thought about that before they built it. They just didn't think anyone could climb these hills. Indians knew they could."

"Thank you Running Bear," Bass said, "we appreciate you showing us how to approach this fort from the backside. It saved us from getting shot up. In the meantime, we need to get back down the hill and get our other horses and the wagons and go pick up these outlaws. Heck, you and Bud probably should stay up here until we get down by the fort, just in case someone else tries to leave before we get down there."

Nobody had tried to leave the fort by the time that Bass and Pittcock and Running Bear got down there. When they got there, they started looking through the bodies to see who they had shot. They had 10 men who had $5,000 rewards each. They stood to collect as much as $60,000. All the outlaws would be covered by the warrants they had from Judge Parker. They found Bob Dalton, who they knew had a $10,000 reward, but they didn't find Jesse James. He must've been the one whose horse Bass had killed and he must've managed to get another horse and get away. "Dang it!" Bass yelled. "We let Jesse James get away. When the others get down here, maybe they can tell us which way he went. I think he was riding the first horse and was about 350 yards away when I took aim on him, but shot his horse. Maybe he was too far away for them to shoot by the time he got on another horse."

When Heck Thomas and Bud Kell arrived with the wagons and their extra horses, Bass asked them "Did you see a man ride away while we were on our way down here?"

"Yep," Bud Kell responded, "there was one of them who got up and chased a horse down and then rode across the river. He was just too far to shoot, even with a rifle, from where we were. He had to be about 600 yards by the time he got to that horse. The way that horse could run, I would say it was probably one of Belle's horses."

"It must've been the horse that Bob Dalton was riding before I shot him." Bass said.

"Probably so." Bud answered. "By now, he would have such a head start that you probably couldn't catch him."

"You're probably right," Bass replied, "I guess Jesse will live for a while longer. We'll have to catch him another day, if the Indians don't kill him before he reaches Mexico. Speaking of Mexico, what do you think we should do about those Mexican women they had with them?"

"They got here on their own," Pittcock said, "let 'em get back to Mexico on their own. We've got plenty to take care of as it is. We can leave them some horses. We've got two men who're still alive, but they'll likely die before we get back to a doctor. We'll just have to throw them in the wagon with the dead men."

"I guess you're right," Bass said, "we don't have much choice, with 9 dead men and 2 wounded. Let's start loading 'em into the wagon. We have a long trip back to Fort Smith. I guess we were lucky they didn't have more men with 'em. By the way, please don't ever tell Belle I accidentally killed one of her horses." They all agreed to that.

After loading the prison wagon, the marshals went back to the fort to load the 6 dead men inside the fort and to look around and make sure they'd not missed anyone. The Mexican women were screaming and crying and acting hysterical, thinking the marshals were going to kill them, but none of them had guns. None of the marshals spoke Spanish, so they had no idea what the women were saying.

"Bass," Bud Kell said, smiling, "as officers of the law, we should confiscate all of this whiskey to make sure it doesn't get in the wrong hands."

"I don't drink," Bass said, "so you can confiscate my share. I would wait until we get back to Fort Smith before drinking any of that. Judge Parker doesn't like to see his marshals drink while they're on the job."

The marshals gathered up the whiskey and found a place for it in the cook wagon. They gathered up all of the firearms and ammunition they could find. They'd sell the pistols and horses and saddles to pay for the outlaws to be buried. They'd keep all of the whiskey and ammunition and some of the rifles. They tied the outlaws' horses to the back of the prison and cook wagons and began the trip back up the Cimarron into Kansas and on to Fort Supply and eventually Fort Smith.

By the time the marshals reached Fort Supply, the wounded men in the prison wagon had died. They got the local mortician to wrap the men's bodies so they wouldn't stink so bad.

By the time the marshals rode into Fort Smith, with a wagon full of dead men, the stink was so bad that the usual crowd kept their distance. They were also disappointed that there wouldn't be a hanging.

The marshals were eager to turn the bodies over for burial. The marshals had photos made together with Bob

Dalton first. Judge Parker verified that all the men had been with Bob Dalton and Jesse James at the time of the train robbery. The Missouri, Kansas and Texas Rail Road replied that they'd be more than happy to pay the $60,000 in rewards for the killing of the gang and Bob Dalton. The marshals would bank $15,000 each for the trip. They'd made more dangerous trips for far less money, but they were bone tired by the time they got back to Fort Smith. It'd been a long hard trip.

"We need to go on more of these trips with you, Bass," Heck said, "then we could all retire pretty soon." The men all laughed at that.

9

THE UPBRINGING

Bass was sitting on the front porch one afternoon, smoking his pipe, when his oldest son, Robert walked up to him and said "Poppa, I've met a girl who lives in Van Buren and we're thinking about getting married. I've brought her up here to the ranch and momma has approved of her. I want to be able to buy a house in town and raise my own family."

"Well son," Bass replied, "I figured I would be losing you and maybe Sallie, pretty soon. What can I do to help you?"

"Poppa, I've decided that I want to be a Deputy U.S. Marshal like you. Would you be O.K. with that and would you be willing to teach me how to be a marshal?"

"Son," Bass said, "the choice of how you make your living is up to you. I know we taught you how to be a blacksmith, and you're good with horses, but if you want to be a marshal, I'd be happy to teach you. Have you talked to your mother about this?"

"Yessir," Robert said, "and she's not very happy about it, but she said the same as you, that I was a grown man and it was up to me to decide."

"Well," Bass said, "I have one more trip to make before the Washington-McLish trial, so you can start your training by going with me on that trip. There are two brothers I heard about who each have a $5,000 reward on their heads. If we can kill or capture them, I'd split that with you and that'd be enough to buy you a house and give you a 'nest egg'. Have you already picked out a house?"

"Susan's found one she likes in Van Buren," Robert said, "Susan Brady is my future wife's name."

"Well, I can train you to be a marshal," Bass said, "and I hope you'll also help me keep an eye on the horses and pastures we have outside Van Buren."

"I'd love to do that," Robert said, "I still love taking care of horses. And I'd want to keep shoeing horses for you when you need that."

"That'd be great," Bass said. "we can leave tomorrow morning, if you can leave then. Maybe we can go by the house you're looking at on our way to Fort Smith."

"Yes sir," Robert said, "we can leave tomorrow if that suits you."

"That'll be good," Bass said, "we can get Green to saddle you one of the thoroughbreds that I bought from Belle Starr. I'm going to ride Ruby."

"Thanks, Poppa," Robert said, "you have a horse named Ruby?" He couldn't help but laugh at that. "You have a horse named Ruby?" he asked again. Bass looked over at Robert with a frown and said,

"Don't be telling everybody about my horse being named Ruby," Bass said, pretending to be mad, "I might have to whip you."

"Don't worry, Poppa," Robert said, kind of worried, "I won't say a word to anyone."

Bass laughed and said "I'm just kidding, son, but I really hope you don't make a big deal out of the horse's name. I bought her from Belle Starr and that was her name before I bought her. Belle made me promise not to change her name."

Robert laughed, relieved that his dad wasn't mad at him. "Well, I'm sure it's a pretty horse." he said.

"And very fast," Bass said, "so you'll have a hard time keeping up, if I let her go full speed." They both began to laugh. Everytime Robert thought about the horse's name, he laughed about it. He just couldn't help it.

The next day, they saddled up and headed down the hill to Van Buren. Robert took him to the house that Susan had picked out. It was on the edge of town and was on about 100 acres. Robert told him that it was going to be for sale pretty soon.

"I think this is the place that Green Saunders was talking about," Bass said, "I'd already told him to buy it to add to our pastureland. It touches our other land on one side. If he buys it, we can deed the house to you."

"Great," Robert said, "the house needs some fixing up, but Susan really likes it, and she likes living out of the middle of town and I really like the idea of living next to the 100 acres. We could build some stables on it if we need to."

"That works for me," Bass said, "it will serve both our purposes well."

After they rode through Fort Smith, Bass took Robert in to see Marshal Boles. "Marshal Boles, I believe you've met my oldest son, Robert. He just turned 20 years old and is getting married pretty soon to Susan Brady, from Van Buren. She's a school teacher who can read and write and is pretty smart, according to what Robert told me on the way over here. Robert wants to be a Deputy U.S. Marshal, like me, and I was wondering if you had any openings and if you'd consider him. I've taught him to shoot and ride a horse and I can train him to be a good marshal. He can ride as good as any man I know and I think he'd make you a good marshal."

"Boy," Marshal Boles began, "do you think you could stand face to face with an evil outlaw and draw your gun and kill him without thinking?"

"Sir," Robert replied, "I'm not sure if I can do that or not. The only way to find out for sure is to let me try. I'll be the loser if I cannot. My Susan would be a widow. I'm sure I don't want to make her a widow. I think I can do it. My poppa is willing to teach me how to survive against such men. If he can't teach me, then I don't know who could. I'm willing to risk my life, if you're willing to risk hiring me."

"Well," Marshal Boles said, "at least you're giving me an honest answer. And you're right, there's no better man to teach you how to be a marshal than Bass. I do need another man or two and I'm willing to give you a chance. Lift your right hand in the air and place your left hand on this bible and repeat after me. I solemnly swear…"

"I solemnly swear…" Robert repeated.

"that I will uphold the laws of the United States of America…" Boles continued.

"that I will uphold the laws of the United States of America…" Robert repeated.

"and uphold the bidding of Judge Parker's Court…" Boles continued.

"and uphold the bidding of Judge Parker's Court…" Robert repeated.

"so help me God." Boles finished.

"so help me God." Robert ended.

Boles pinned a Deputy U.S. Marshal's badge on Robert's shirt and said,

"Congratulations deputy."

Robert was thrilled, even though he knew this was just the beginning. The hardest part was still in front of him. He couldn't wait to return and show Susan his badge. She'd be so proud of him. He'd told her what he intended to do and she was pleased. She served the needs of her children in school and she'd be proud that he was serving the law.

"Congratulations Son!" Bass said, holding back the tears that were trying to form in his eyes as best he could. This was one of the proudest moments of Bass's life. He hated to see Robert leave his home, but knew he'd still be nearby. He'd known this time would come.

"Thanks, Poppa," Robert said, "I'm excited."

"From now on," Bass said, "you'll address me as Marshal Reeves, not Poppa."

"Yes sir, Po... I mean Marshal Reeves." Robert said. Calling him Poppa would be a hard habit to break.

"I'll call you Marshal Rob." Bass said.

"Okay Marshal Reeves." Robert replied.

"Come on, Marshal Rob," Bass said, "I want to take you to see the greatest man I've ever met and introduce him to his newest marshal."

Walking into Judge Parker's office, Bass boomed out in a loud voice, "Judge Isaac Parker, I'd like to introduce you to Deputy U.S. Marshal Robert Reeves!"

The judge almost got tears in his eyes when he saw how proud Bass was of his son. "So your boy has decided to join you in the enforcement of the law?" Judge Parker said. "That's a very good thing, because you're getting so old, we probably ought to be putting you out to pasture pretty soon." the judge said, laughing out loud, "we needed to get you a replacement. Boy, you've got some really big boots to fill.

"Yessir," Robert replied, "they are big boots, but I can already wear 'em."

"Well," Judge Parker said, "that's a good thing! Congratulations to both of you! I couldn't be happier. Of course, any marshal who is appointed has to be approved by me before he's allowed to go out and face the bad guys, but I do approve of you Robert! Just try not to let Bass get you killed before you get more experience. You know that not just everyone wants to ride with him. He goes after the really bad guys."

"That's what pays the most money," Bass said, "and that's why I do it. If you're going to risk your life, it might as well be for the most money you can get. Besides, the baddest men are the ones that need killing. They are usually murderers or rapists or train robbers or horse thieves or all of those put together. And the Indian Nation is full of men like that. "

"That's for sure," Judge Parker said, "and that's why this court was put here by the President himself. We have to protect the law-abiding Indians and white people and colored people from the bad guys, who don't abide by the law. The Lighthorse can't arrest anyone that's not an Indian, so they depend on us to help them, and we depend on them to help us. One of the reasons your dad is so effective, Robert, is that he is loved and respected by the Indians and he can speak all of their languages. So it would be good for you to learn to speak their languages. They'll give you respect because of your name. But they'll expect you to live up to that name. Do you understand that?"

"Yessir," Robert said. "I already know how to speak Creek and Cherokee, because my mother taught me, and I speak Creek to the Indians who work on our ranch."

"That's good," Judge Parker said, "you'll need those skills. Bass can teach you how to survive out there."

"Yessir," Robert replied, "Marshal Reeves has promised me he'll show me how to stay alive for my Susan."

Judge Parker was amused that Robert was calling Bass 'Marshal Reeves'. He guessed that was what he was told to do. If the boy did what he was told to do, he would become a great lawman like his dad. He had no doubt that would happen.

Soon, Bass and Robert were ready to leave Fort Smith and head to Indian Territory. Bass had heard the 2 outlaw brothers they were after were from an area near Fort Towson, on a ranch on Little River, not far from the Texas border. It was about 150 miles from Fort Smith and would take about 5 days to ride there. A Choctaw Lighthorse had told Marshal Boles when he was in Fort Smith that the brothers had been seen at the ranch. It was believed their mother was helping them to hide in the area.

Bass had decided to ride south to Broken Bow and then head west to the ranch. They would be in the Choctaw Nation most of the way and he knew most of the Lighthorse in that area. He also spoke Choctaw and was always recognized as a friend of the Indians there. His only worry was how to capture the brothers.

When they reached Broken Bow, Bass told Robert that his plan was to obtain a map to the ranch from the Lighthorse and then to hide the cook wagon and the prison wagon as close to the ranch as possible. Then he planned to disguise himself as a fugitive and approach the house on foot. Robert thought that was crazy.

"You're taking a big chance going to that ranch house on foot," Robert said, "what if they come after you and you have no horse? They could easily catch you. Why don't we go in there together?"

"Marshal Rob," Bass began, "I'm the one training you. I'm going to show you how you can capture outlaws without ever firing a shot, by using your head instead of your gun. But I'll take my guns. They'll just be hidden under a loose fittin' jacket. Don't worry, I can take care of any two outlaws out there. I've done it before."

"Okay," Robert said, "but I'm going to be waiting with two horses saddled and ready. If I hear any shots, I'm going to come riding to you."

"That's fine," Bass said, "but I don't think I'll need you to do that."

After they got the map to the ranch from a Lighthorse policeman, they made the ride from Broken Bow. It was afternoon before they got to a small patch of woods in some foothills of the Kiamichi Mountains, where Bass figured he could walk to the ranch before dark. He'd brought some loose fitting raggedy clothes to wear and had brought a hat with a few bullet holes in it from a previous gunfight.

Robert watched him as he walked down the hills towards the ranch. Robert guessed he had better get used to seeing his poppa in danger. That's what he did for a living. He had a new respect for his father now that he was close to the danger of the job. At that moment, he vowed he'd become a better lawman so that he wouldn't be a burden to his father. He wanted to become an asset to his father and wanted Bass to be proud of him. He still couldn't help but worry as he waited. Bass had told him that it might be the next morning when he returned.

When Bass reached the farmhouse, a woman stepped out on the front porch with a double barreled shotgun pointed straight at him. "What do you want?" she demanded. "What're you doing here?" He knew that one wrong move would result in a load of shot heading for him.

"Ma'am," Bass said, in an humble voice, "I'm just a poor colored man who's down on his luck. Some lawmen just shot at me this afternoon and put holes in my hat and shot my horse," he said, holding the hat out for her to see, "I just need to hide somewhere and I'm awful hungry. I'd cut you some firewood if you'd share some food with me."

"Why should I let some outlaw colored man come into my home?"

"Ma'am," Bass said in a wavering voice, "I stole some money from a store in Broken Bow and I have some silver dollars I could give you for a meal."

"How many silver dollars do you have," she asked, seemingly interested in making a trade, "and how many of them will I get to feed you?"

"I would give you 3 dollars for a meal and a place to stay tonight. It looks like it could rain soon and I don't have no shelter."

"Show me the money," the woman demanded, "I don't believe you have 3 dollars."

Bass fished in his pocket and pulled out 3 silver dollars and held them up.

"Come on in," the woman said, lowering the shotgun and taking the money, "I just got through cooking dinner."

When Bass entered the house, he saw a table with 6 chairs that had 3 plates set. "You must have expected me to be here," Bass said, "but who's the other plate for?"

"Don't be a smart ass!" the woman said, gesturing with the shotgun, "sit down at the table and I'll put some food out. Those two plates I put out were for my two sons, who are supposed to be here any minute. If you don't behave right, they'll fill your head with holes to match your hat." Bass did as he was told and sat down to one of the plates. The woman set another place at the table. She was starting to put food on the table, when they heard a loud whistle out back. She went out back with the shotgun and when she returned, she had two men with her.

"Who the hell is this guy?" one of the men asked, drawing his pistol and pointing it at Bass.

"He's some outlaw that offered me 3 dollars to eat dinner and stay the night." the woman answered, "I don't see you offering me 3 dollars for dinner and a stay."

"That's real funny." the man with his gun drawn said, "Who the hell are you?" He asked Bass.

"I'm jus' a poor outlaw colored man who got hisself shot at by the law and they killed my horse." Bass said, "But I have enough silver dollars to buy a horse. I stole it from a store in Broken Bow."

"Lemme see the money," the man with his gun drawn said. Bass pulled a bag full of silver coins out of his pocket. "How much money is there?" the other man asked.

"Should be close to $100 in silver coins in there." Bass answered.

"What's your name?" The man with the gun on him said.

"Hellubee Sammy." Bass answered.

"That's a hell of a name." The man with the gun said. "My name is Joe and this man with me is my brother Jasper. This woman is our momma."

"Pleased to meet you." Bass responded.

"We have an extra horse we can sell you," Joe said. "He ain't much, but we just killed his owner, so he ain't gonna need his horse any more. He even had a rifle in a scabbard we'll kick in. We can let you have the horse and rifle for $75."

"I think I'll jus' take you up on that," Bass said, "with a horse and rifle, I can get more money. If I see those lawmen again, I'll put them under the dirt."

"We're gettin' ready to ride down to Texas and maybe rob a bank or train." Joe said, "We'll be leaving tomorrow, do you wanna go with us?"

"Why sure." Bass said. "I may go on down to Mexico if we can get us a bunch of money."

"That's what we plan on doin'." Jasper said.

"You can bunk down in the stable after dinner." The woman said.

"We can all sleep in the bunk room," Joe said, "there's 3 beds in there."

"You sure?" His momma said.

"I'm sure." Joe said. He wanted to be able to keep an eye on this guy. He wasn't sure that he trusted him yet.

Once they got on the horses, they would be close to each other and if he went for the rifle, they could easily outdraw him with pistols.

After dinner, they all slept in their clothes on the bottoms of 3 bunk beds. Bass was barely able to sleep all night, because he was worried they might try to jump him while he was sleeping.

The next morning, after a good breakfast, the three men mounted their horses. The horses already had saddles on them. Bass thought to himself that was a careless way to leave a horse all night, but these were careless people.

After they had ridden a short distance from the ranch house, Bass quickly threw back the bottom of his jacket and drew his pistols. The other men started to draw their pistols, but saw that Bass had the advantage, so they raised their hands in the air instead.

"I'm Bass Reeves, a Deputy U.S. Marshal, and you men are under arrest. Slowly take your pistols out of the holster with two fingers and drop them on the ground."

"You son-of-a-bitch," Joe said.

"You can keep your sentiments to yourself," Bass allowed, "if you say another word, you're a dead man. Now, get down off your horses very slowly and drop your reins on the ground." Once he had them on the ground, he tied their hands behind their backs, picked up their pistols and made them walk several miles back to where Robert and the wagons were hiding.

"I see the plan worked," Robert said as Bass rode up, "me and the cook were getting worried."

"No need to worry," Bass said, "I've been doing this for a long time. I just wanted to show you that you don't always have to be the fastest gun to take an outlaw. Sometimes you just have to use your head.

"I can see that," Robert said, "did you have to outdraw them?"

"Naw," Bass answered, "I just caught them off guard and drew my pistols when they weren't paying attention. They thought the only gun I had was the rifle in a scabbard on the horse I bought from them. By the way, get that $75 out of their pockets before you put 'em in the prison wagon. That's my money I gave 'em for this poor excuse for a horse."

"That is a pretty sorry horse." Robert said. "It looked like it could barely hold you up."

Bass laughed about that, "This poor thing was wobbling all the way over here. I thought sure it was going to fall over, but it made it. I'll be glad to get back on Ruby."

"Ruby?" Jasper said, breaking out in laughter, "that's your horses name, Ruby?" Joe couldn't help but laugh at that himself. They sounded like a couple of jackasses.

"I told you I was going to kill you if you said another word!" Bass said as he drew both his guns and aimed them at the men. They both shut up quickly. Meanwhile, Robert and the cook had started laughing.

"Darn it!" Bass said to Robert, "I'm going to regret buying that horse. I may just give it to Susan as a wedding present when you two get married."

"I think that's a real good idea," Robert said, "she'd really like that horse."

"But I still want to breed her to my stallions, and get some offspring out of the deal." Bass said.

"That's a deal!" Robert said.

After 5 days of travel, they were riding up the east bank of the Poteau River just south of Fort Smith, when Bass turned north to cross the Poteau and head towards the Arkansas River. Normally, they would have ridden up the Poteau River to where it joined the Arkansas near Fort Smith.

"Where are we going," Robert asked, "aren't we going back to Fort Smith?"

"There's one other thing we need to do," Bass said, "before we go to Fort Smith. One of the Cherokee Nation Lighthorse asked me to meet him on the north side of the Arkansas River at the crossing into the Cherokee Nation. He's been talkin' to Indians who've been buying whiskey and he thinks there's a big shipment of whiskey headed to the Cherokee Nation from Fort Smith. He thinks they're going to cross the river tonight after dark. We should get there about an hour before dark."

"Will there be any shooting?" Robert asked. He was beginning to think he wasn't going to get to use his guns on this trip. He'd been given a twin holster rig just like his dad's with the gun handles pointing forward for his 18th birthday and he'd been practicing drawing his pistols every day since. He was getting faster.

"I imagine so," Bass said, "there'll be a full moon tonight, but it'll still hard to see what you're shooting at. Just don't shoot me."

"You know I won't be shooting at you," Robert said, "I've been practicing drawing and shooting every day."

"I know," Bass said, "but I've seen people do some funny things when they get in a gunfight... I saw one man shoot himself in the foot when he was trying to draw on me one time! That was the funniest thing I'd ever seen! I don't think he liked me laughing at him, but I just couldn't help it." Robert laughed at the thought.

"That's not going to happen with me." Robert said.

"We'll see." Bass said. It was true that you never knew what people would do when guns started blazing around them. He was training another young marshal, when an outlaw shot at them, and the young marshal took off running to his horse, rode away, and never came back. He laughed again just thinking about that.

"What are you laughing at?" Robert asked.

"Nothing important." Bass said.

After they had crossed the Poteau River and the Arkansas River, they rode to where they were supposed to meet the Lighthorse, Joseph Whitehorse. He was there as promised. He spoke in Cherokee to Bass, and Robert understood most of what he said.

"Hello brother. Who's this young man with you?"

"This is my son Robert," Bass responded in Cherokee.

"Nice to meet you." Robert spoke up in Cherokee.

"Robert, you'll soon be brother of Cherokee also." Whitehorse responded. "Bass," he continued, "I've been counting the days of shipments across the river and if the schedule hasn't been changed, this is the day of the moon when they should be bringing firewater to the Cherokee. I can't arrest 'em, because they're all white people."

"I know you have no jurisdiction and that's why I promised to meet you here," Bass said. "I figured we would have finished our business by now. How many guards do they usually bring with them?"

"They usually bring two wagons across at a time. Each wagon usually has one guard with a shotgun and one rider on a horse with a rifle. They all have 6-guns. Once they cross the river they head northwest towards Fort Gibson. I figured you could take them down as soon as they cross the river," Whitehorse said.

"I can make you a temporary posse man," Bass said, "if you want to help us take them into custody. We could use the extra gunpowder."

"It'd be my pleasure to serve as your posse man," Whitehorse answered, "I'm able to take a man with a rifle out to 200 yards."

"I figure we should stay over here by these cottonwood trees until they cross," Bass said, "and then the first wagon should be about 100 yards away by the time the second wagon clears the river. Those shotguns won't be much use at that distance. I figure when they get that close, I'll shout out that we're U.S. Marshals and command them to drop their weapons.

If they don't drop their weapons, Whitehorse, I figure you should take out the closest man with a rifle and I'll take out the farthest man with a rifle. Robert, I want you to shoot the closest man with a shotgun, then try to shoot the man in the second wagon with the shotgun. If we take care of business, it should be over in a few minutes."

"Should we wait until they shoot at us before we start shooting?" Robert asked.

"Son, I've stayed alive this long by shooting first and asking questions later. Judge Parker said if they're breaking the law and carrying guns and refuse to drop the guns when asked, we shoot first. This isn't a fast draw contest or a turkey shoot. This is our job. Most of the people we go after are wanted dead or alive. We get paid either way. If they turn and run, you don't have to shoot them, but most likely they'll return fire if they can. This territory is full of rats. We need to clean 'em out."

"Yessir, Marshal Reeves." Robert responded. He wasn't sure he could shoot a man without him being shot at first, but he'd see.

About an hour after dark, they could see the wagons crossing the river. It was a really crisp clear night and the skies were lit up good enough to see the men, but it would be hard to see their gunsights. They would have to trust their instincts. When the wagons cleared the river, they waited for Bass to tell the men to drop their weapons.

"This is Bass Reeves, U.S. Marshal! Drop your weapons!" The gunmen raised their weapons and started to fire in their direction.

"Shoot 'em," Bass shouted, "don't let anyone get away." The men started shooting as commanded. Bass killed the farthest man with a rifle, about 300 yards away. Whitehorse killed the closest man with a rifle and Robert shot the closest wagon guard who had a shotgun. By that time, the second wagon turned and headed up the river away from them.

"Go get him!" Bass hollered at Robert, "don't let 'em get away. Whitehorse, go stop that first wagon!" The first wagon had turned around and was heading back to the river. Whitehorse managed to get the first wagon stopped. The driver did not draw his pistol and surrendered.

Robert took aff after the furthest wagon. Bass began to follow Robert, but was going to let him take care of the situation if possible. As Robert was chasing the other wagon which was headed towards Fort Gibson. The guard with the shotgun started shooting towards Robert when he was about 60 yards away and he felt some of the pellets strike him in the leg. He returned fire with his rifle and hit the guard on his third shot. When the guard fell out of the wagon, the driver of the wagon stopped and held up his hands. Robert put his rifle back into its scabbard and pulled one of his pistols and aimed it at the man, saying "I'm Robert Reeves, U.S. Marshal, put your hands up, you're under arrest!"

The man raised his hands, while still holding on to the reigns. The horses pulling the wagon were still jumping around and nervous, but they finally settled down. Bass rode up behind him.

"Good job son!" Bass bellowed. Then he noticed there was a dark stain on Robert's light colored pants. "Dangit Boy, did you get shot on your first trip?" Robert looked down at his leg. In all the excitement he hadn't even felt the sting of the shot, but he was beginning to.

"I don't think it's anything but buckshot," Robert replied, "I didn't feel a thing."

"Well," Bass said, "I just hope your mother doesn't hit me with a frying pan for letting you get shot. How many shot got you?" After getting down off his horse and surveying the damage, Robert determined that he caught one buckshot in each leg and his horse had caught one in its neck. The buckshot were only a few inches deep, so Bass pulled them out with his pocketknife, including the one from the horse. In a few minutes he got the bleeding stopped with a compound he carried.

"Let's camp here for the night." Bass suggested, " We can cross the river in the morning." They gathered up all of the dead men and tied two of them to horses and put the other two in the wagons. Bass figured they would be okay until the morning. Whitehorse told Bass he would like to go on home, if Bass did not need him in the morning. So Bass thanked him and told him to go ahead and go home. He then tied the wagon drivers up and they bedded down for the night.

"Good night Marshal Rob." Bass said.

"Good night Marshal Reeves." Robert answered.

10

THE TRIAL OF BILLY WASHINGTON AND DICK MCLISH

It was an unusual scene as the marshals crossed the Arkansas River the next morning and rode down Garrison Avenue before turning to the courthouse and jail. There were the two marshals, a cook wagon, a prison wagon with the two brothers, then two large covered wagons with drivers tied to the wagon seat, with a dead man in each covered wagon and then two dead men tied to two horses that were tied to the wagons.

Marshal Boles met them as they approached the jail. "How did my new deputy marshal do on his first trip?"

Bass replied "He didn't take off and run, at least not until I told him to. But he went and got himself shot on his first trip."

"What?" Boles asked "He doesn't look like he's been shot… oh now I see, it looks like he got shot in the leg."

"He got shot in both legs." Bass allowed. "And he got the horse he was riding shot!"

"Well, that's a heck of a first trip!" Boles said. "He may not want to go on another trip with you, Bass. That's not the first time you got one of your new marshals shot!"

"You didn't have to bring that up!" Bass said. "Are you trying to scare the boy off?"

"No," Boles said, "He just might prefer to be trained by a marshal who doesn't take so many risks."

Robert laughed and said, "I'm okay, I just caught a buckshot in each leg. Marshal Reeves has already removed the lead. I should be good to go in a few days."

"Well," Boles continued, "don't try to be a tough guy, you should go let the doctor put something on the wounds."

"Yessir, Marshal Boles," Robert replied…he would do what he was told.

"Bass," Boles said, "when you get through puttin' all of these men in jail and takin' care of the wagons and such, we need to talk about the Washington and McLish trial. It'll be coming up in a few more days and we need to make sure we have all of the witnesses lined up for the trial and Judge Parker wants to discuss it with you before you go on home."

"I'll come by your office and go see Judge Parker in about an hour." Bass replied. "Marshal Rob, you can go home after we're finished. Check with Green Saunders and see if he bought that house and 100 acres while we were gone. You've got $5,000 to set you up in marriage. I'll put it in the bank until you need it."

"Thanks Marshal Reeves!" Robert said. "Do I get to keep any of the whiskey?"

"Boy," Bass said, "you'd better be kiddin' about that whiskey. Your momma would tear you up, even if you are full grown, if she saw you drinking any whiskey! Besides, that whiskey is evidence."

"I was just kidding!" Robert said.

Robert was excited to get home and see if Green Saunders had managed to buy the property with the house that Susan wanted.

Meanwhile, Bass made the visit to Judge Parker's office. "Morning Judge," Bass said, "did you want to see me?"

"We need to talk about this upcoming trial," Judge Parker said, "and I wanted to ask you how our new marshal did on his first trip."

"Well," Bass said, "as I told Marshal Boles, the boy didn't run, but he did get hisself shot a couple of times."

"Really?" Judge Parker said, "How bad?"

"Not too bad," Bass said, "he just caught a couple of buckshot in his legs and his horse caught one too, but they were only inside the flesh about an inch or so. I dug 'em out with my pocket knife. Boles told him to go get Doc to look at 'em. He killed the guard who shot him, and it didn't seem to bother him to shoot somebody."

"Well, I'm glad you didn't get him killed on his first day," Judge Parker said, "like you did with that Jasper Stone kid."

"You didn't have to bring that up Judge," Bass said, "that wasn't my fault. The kid ran and got shot in the back. I couldn't help that."

"I know," the Judge laughed, "but I just couldn't let you forget it."

"I haven't forgotten it," Bass said, "I felt pretty bad about it. Especially havin' to tell his parents. I understood how they felt. Also, Judge, the crates with the whiskey in them came from a liquor distributor located here in Fort Smith. I think Washington owns part of it.

"Do you think those wagon drivers will testify that the whiskey came from there?" Judge Parker asked.

"I don't know," Bass said, "I'd get Boles to see if he can get 'em to testify."

"I'll ask Boles to look into that. Washington will be madder than a wet hen just because they lost all that whiskey," Judge Parker said. "Right now, we have an attempted murder charge to worry about. He and Dick McLish's trial is coming up in two more days. We still have that witness, John Bruner, that you brought in who's in jail. Is that Indian who worked for McLish still around to testify?"

"Yessir," Bass answered, "but I don't think he speaks real good English. We may need an interpreter, besides me, to tell the jury what he's saying."

"That won't be a problem," the Judge said, "we have another marshal who can speak Creek. He'll be in town. I don't want you to leave on another trip until this trial is over with. I'll need your sister and her husband to testify about Fred Cobb coming up to your place and buying those horses and the Indian guard who was on duty when he came up. The prosecuting attorney, William H. H. Clayton, will want to review the case with all of them and you should consult with him about what he expects to do. As I understand it, Thomas Marcum has agreed to defend Washington and McLish. As you know, he is a partner in the Clayton, Cravens and Marcum law firm."

"Do you expect it to be a fair trial when the prosecuter is in the same law practice as the person defending them?" Bass asked.

"We don't have much choice," Judge Parker said, "in a small town with 3 good lawyers. They're often against each other. It might not seem right, but that's just the way it is. They know better than to try to pull anything unfair in my court. And you know, I suggested you use the same law firm in your trial."

"I guess if attorney Marcum does a good job of defending Washington and McLish, I should use him in my trial," Bass said "since there isn't much choice."

"Probably so," Judge Parker said, "he's probably the strongest lawyer in town. Clayton is a hard prosecutor, so you'll need the best you can get."

The two days passed and it was time for the trial. There was a big crowd in the courtroom, including the newspaper editor, Bart Simms.

"Oh yes! Oh yes! The Honorable District and Circuit Courts of the United States for the Western District of Arkansas, having criminal jurisdiction of the Indian Territory is now in session! All rise!"

Judge Parker walked into the courtroom in his official robe and declared the court in session for the trial of Billy Washington and Dick McLish. He then began his charge to the jury:

"Gentlemen of the Jury, before proceeding with this trial, I desire to address to you a few remarks by way of a reminder of what your duties are under the law. That reminder has already been given to you in the shape of your oath, which is an epitome of the great duties that devolve upon you as the power of the government in this district, for this term of court. But it is sometimes considered to be more impressive and we are more apt to understand our duties, when we can converse for a brief time about them.

I never open a term of court that I am not impressed again and again with the greatness of this government of ours. Its greatness consists in the fact that all of its power is in the hands of those who are to be benefited or injured by the execution or the neglect to execute that great power… in the hands of the people themselves. In the first place, the laws are made by their agents. They are made for their protection, to secure their rights and when they do not bring to them that protection, and do not secure to them these rights, they are bad laws. They are vicious laws. No good citizen should ever let his partisan opinions or his political views, no matter what party he belongs to, run so high as to forget the great truth of the principle as to what his duty may be as to the government of his country and its laws.

Now, what I have said is based upon the fact that laws are worthless to protect the rights of the people unless they are executed. The laws of the United States can not be executed in this district until you, as a jury, first act in the premises. You occupy such a position as that the government through its officer comes to you and says: 'I present this man, or that, or other, and convict them of a crime.' The government is the charging power. The government brings this case before you.

Before any action can be taken to punish that person, you must ascertain finally the guilt or innocence of that person. The evidence is presented to you through the district attorney, or some one of his assistants, and you pass upon the question primarily as to whether he is guilty or innocent.

We have but to cite this fact to show the great responsibilities that rest upon you, to show you the importance of the position you assume or that is cast upon you. That is why you are brought here. It is a principle of law, arising under the Constitution of the United States, that if a man is the accused of a crime, it must be heard by you.

By finding a verdict of guilty where guilt exists, you are doing your duty, and also are teaching one of the greatest object lessons. Judging from the vast volume of crime, which has almost submerged us in a sea of blood, we have gone astray and are almost at the mercy of the man of crime. The greatest question of the hour is, can we properly enforce the law?

Crime is gaining strength, especially those crimes affecting human life. This is not caused entirely by the failure of the people to enforce the laws. There are other causes and sources. One of our leading newspapers, in commenting upon this case, asserting that the defendants are innocent of any crime, has set the tone for a great injustice. Let this jury ignore such ignorant and biased articles that may be printed in this newspaper as simply trash that litters the street. Although our freedom of speech is also one of our treasured rights under our system of government, that right should not be carelessly abused.

You will bear in mind that there is a veil of secrecy thrown around your proceedings. You are not to make known what proceedings are transpiring in the jury room to anybody on the outside; you are not to inform anyone what you are doing. Nor are you permitted to make known how any member of your body votes upon a proposition, or what opinions he expresses upon questions that may be pending before you."

With that charge, he turned the trial over to the Prosecuting Attorney, William H. H. Clayton for his opening remarks:

"The defendants, Billy Washington and Dick McLish, seated here before you," Clayton began, "have been charged with setting forth others in their employ, to attempt to murder U.S. Marshal Bass Reeves and to attempt to murder members of Marshal Reeves' family. This court is horrified by these apparent actions and intends to prove these charges and prosecute the defendants to the full extent of the law. It is alleged that defendants placed posters in and around Muskogee, Indian Territory, soliciting gunmen to come into their employ, at a fee of $500 each, and were offered a reward of $5,000 to be split amongst them, in the event they have success in their charge. We have introduced copies of these posters, which were taken off posts in the area of one of the saloons in Muskogee, as evidence against these defendants. You will hear from Marshal Reeves about his encounters with the men selected and paid by the defendants and you will hear from one of the men, who is still alive, who was a part of that group of outlaws working for the defendants.

You will also hear from Marshal Reeves regarding his encounter with this group and the results thereof. You will hear testimony from the Town Sheriff in Muskogee regarding the placement of the subject posters around the city of Muskogee soliciting gunmen for the period of time in question. This jury will also hear testimony that the defendants sent one of their men, Fred Cobb, to buy horses from Marshal Reeves' ranch and used that opportunity to determine a plan to attempt to kill Marshal Reeves' family, who live at that location.

You will hear testimony from Marshal Bass Reeves, Marshals J.H. Mershon, William P. Pittcock, Bud Kell and Heck Thomas as to a shootout that took place at Marshal Reeves' ranch, in which they killed the men sent to harm Marshal Reeves' family. As stated by Judge Parker, it is your duty to consider this evidence and render justice in this matter. It is the opinion of this prosecutor that we will prove the guilt of these defendants without a shadow of doubt."

It was then the turn of Thomas Marcum, who was defending Billy Washington and Dick McLish:

"Gentlemen of the jury, my clients, Mr. Billy Washington and Mr. Dick McLish are prominent ranchers at a sizable ranch that is near Muskogee. They are good citizens, who have never been charged with a crime. They are forced to hire gunmen, from time to time, to protect their livestock and possessions. They do not deny they have placed posters seeking gunmen. They will testify that they have never conspired to harm Marshal Reeves or any of his relatives.

Fred Cobb will testify that he has been to Marshal Reeves' ranch and has no idea why anyone would have an idea that he was up to no good. In fact, he did business at Bass Reeves' ranch and purchased horses there. In the end, we will prove that the events that Marshal Reeves claims were motivated by my clients were unrelated to their actions whatsoever and exist only in the mind of Marshal Reeves and his marshal friends.

It is in fact a theory that cannot be proven in a court of law and that is what we intend to prove. My clients do not know why Marshal Reeves has decided that he will harm them or their reputation with such made up accusations. They only wish to get back to the business of running their ranch and to be left alone to do that. They are aggravated to be charged with such crimes and may be inclined to sue Marshal Reeves himself."

Next, Bass Reeves testified as to the first incident and he testified as follows: "Your honor, there were two men that I'd been searching for who were rumored to be in Muskogee and had been seen in a saloon. So I went to the saloon and walked in the door and stated to the people in the saloon, 'I am Bass Reeves, Deputy U.S. Marshal and I'm looking for a man named Frank Buck and a man named John Bruner. They are both negros who're wanted for horse thievery.' After I'd said that, two colored men stood up and said they knew where the men were and offered to help me find them for $100. I left the saloon with the two men, after giving them each $100 in silver coins, and they led me to a small stream where we decided to camp for the night.

While I was making coffee, I noticed both men were acting funny and both had their hands on their guns. Then I pretended to go around one of the men, who turned out to be John Bruner, to check on my horse and turned my back on him. When I glanced back over my shoulder, I saw that Bruner was drawing his gun and I made a quick move and grabbed his gun and put my arm around his neck. When I did that, the other man, who turned out to be Frank Buck, went for his gun and I shot him with Bruner's gun. I then tied up Bruner, who told me they'd been hired by Billy Washington to kill me. I then asked him if he'd testify to that in court and he stated that he would. I then tied him up. Then other shots were fired at me out of the dark and I killed one of the gunmen.

I stayed awake all night, hidden between some trees. At daybreak, the other men started shooting at me again. At that time, Bruner told me they were Billy Washington's men and one of them was a former Texas Ranger. I then shot another of the men with my rifle. The last man then left on his horse. I got on my horse but was not able to catch him. It looked like he was headed back towards Texas. His horse flat outran mine. When I got back to where the men had been, I discovered two horses tied to a tree that were two of the horses I had raised back at my ranch. I then suspected the other horse that got away was also one of mine. When I got back to my ranch, my ranch manager, Green Saunders, told me that someone came to my ranch and told Green he was there to buy horses for the army. It was those horses that these men were riding."

"Your witness," Clayton responded to Thomas Marcum.

Marcum began to question Marshal Reeves. "So Marshal Reeves, you had never seen any of these men before you killed them?"

"No sir," Bass responded, "I'd never seen these men before."

"So Marshal Reeves," Marcum continued, "how did you come to the conclusion that these men were hired by my clients?"

"John Bruner told me that." Reeves responded.

"So a horse thief that you had been looking for to arrest, told you that he and the other men had been hired by my clients to kill you?" Marcum asked.

"That's correct," Bass said.

"I thought you said Bruner told you they were hired by Billy Washington?" Marcum stated.

"That's correct." Bass responded.

"So he never told you he was working for Dick McLish?"

"No sir." Bass answered.

"So what made you think he was working for McLish?" Marcum asked.

"They're partners and the posters looking for gunmen said they were from Washington and McLish." Bass said.

"But you were not told by your witness, Mr. Bruner that McLish was involved?" Marcum supposed.

"No sir." Bass answered.

"And did you pay Mr. Bruner $100 to testify against my clients?" Marcum asked Reeves.

"No sir," Bass said, "I paid Bruner $100 when he said he'd lead me to the people I was looking for."

"That is all for Marshal Reeves," Marcum informed the judge, "but I reserve the right to recall this witness."

"So noted." Judge Parker allowed.

The next witness was John Bruner.

"Mr. Bruner," Clayton asked him, "please tell this court how you came to meet the defendants and what they asked you to do."

"Well," Bruner began, "me and Frank Buck had been making a living selling whiskey to the Indians and we had a warrant out for our arrest for stealing some horses. We came across a poster offering $500 a year, paid in advance, to be a gunman for the Washington-McLish ranch and a possible $5 thousand reward. So we went to the ranch and were told by Billy Washington that they'd pay us $500 each in cash and we'd get to split a $5,000 reward if we helped to kill Deputy U.S. Marshal Bass Reeves. It seems like he was mad at Reeves for killing Jim Webb, who had been managing his ranch for him.

"Was Dick McLish in your presence when Billy was making you the offer?" Clayton asked.

"Yes sir," Bruner continued, "They said they sent Fred Cobb to buy some horses from Reeves, so he knew what was going on. They told us to go to town and if the marshal came to town, we were going to offer to help him find the men he was looking for, which would have been us. Then we were going to lead him into an ambush."

"That's all I have for this witness at this time." Clayton told the judge.

"Mr. Bruner," Thomas Marcum asked the witness, "did anyone offer to help you out on your sentence for this crime if you testified against Billy Washington and Dick McLish?"

"Yes sir," Bruner answered, "Marshal Reeves told me he'd see to it that Judge Parker would go easy on me on the horse theft charges and for trying to help kill him, if I'd testify at this trial."

"That's all the questions I have for this witness, your honor," Marcum said, "but I reserve the right to question him again later."

"So noted." Judge Parker said.

"The people would like to call Fred Cobb to the stand, your honor." Clayton said.

When Cobb was called to the stand, Clayton asked him, "Mr. Cobb, how long have you worked for the Washington-McLish ranch?"

"About 5 years." Cobb answered.

"What is your job?" Clayton asked.

"I'm now the ranch manager." Cobb said.

"So you got promoted when Jim Webb was killed by Marshal Reeves?" Clayton surmised.

"Yessir, that's true." Cobb replied.

"Have you ever heard Billy Washington say he would like to see Bass Reeves dead?" Clayton asked.

"No sir." Cobb lied.

"You are aware you are under oath to this court?" Clayton pressed.

"Yessir." Cobb replied.

Clayton asked him again, "You have never heard Billy Washington or Dick McLish discuss killing Bass Reeves or having him killed or having his family killed?"

"No sir." Cobb lied again.

"Did you ever go to Bass Reeves' ranch and pretend to be representing the army and buy horses that belonged to Bass Reeves from his ranch manager Green Saunders?" Clayton asked.

"Yessir." Cobb replied.

"Was one of the purposes of your trip to scout out the Reeves ranch so that others could go try to kill Reeves' family? Clayton asked.

"No sir." Cobb lied again.

"Then why did you lie about being with the army?" Clayton inquired.

"Because Billy didn't think that Reeves would sell us any horses if he knew they were for the Washington-McLish ranch." Cobb lied.

"Your honor," Clayton stated, "I am through with this witness, but I would like the court to note that I do not believe he is telling the truth and that I may wish to recall him at a later time."

"So noted." Judge Parker said while glaring at Cobb. He could tell Cobb was glad to get off the stand. He knew Cobb was lying, but didn't know how they were going to prove it. Maybe the Indian's testimony would help.

"Your honor," Clayton continued, "the people call John Redbird to the stand. John Redbird is a Creek Indian who does not speak a lot of English, so we have a marshal who is going to interpret his testimony."

"That will be fine with this court." Judge Parker replied.

"John Redbird," Clayton said, "could you tell the jury what happened just before you left the employ of the Washington-McLish ranch, and your conversation with Fred Cobb?"

"I can tell you this in English," Redbird said. "I speak much English. Fred Cobb was telling me about plan to get even with Marshal Reeves by killing family. He thought that bad plan. He spoke about going up mountain and tell them how to get to top posing as army. He scared Bass Reeves come kill them all." This brought laughter from the jury until Judge Parker gave them his best glare, while banging his gavel.

"That's when you left the ranch and rode to warn Bass Reeves?" Clayton asked.

"Yes," Redbird replied, "Redbird good friends with Bass's wife Jennie. Not want to see bad men hurt her."

"Your honor," Clayton said, "that is all I have for this witness right now."

"The defense may now cross-examine Mr. Redbird." Judge Parker allowed.

"Mr. Redbird," Thomas Marcum asked, "why did the court provide an interpreter for you?"

"I think," Redbird said, "they not know how much English I speak."

"Did the prosecutor ask you to memorize the statement you made earlier?" Marcum asked.

"Statement from memory." Redbird answered. "Speak much English."

"The prosecutor did not ask you to memorize your statement?"

"No." Redbird answered.

"How are you currently employed?" Marcum asked.

"I work on Bass Reeves' ranch." Redbird responded.

"So Bass Reeves could fire you if he doesn't agree with your testimony?" Marcum asked.

"Redbird not lie!" He responded while jumping out of his seat, as if to lunge at the defense attorney. Marcum jumped back, as if he were being attacked.

"The witness will keep his seat!" Judge Parker growled.

Redbird sat back down, but everyone could tell he was deeply upset.

"Your honor," Marcum said, appearing to calm down, "I am through with this witness, although I reserve the right to re-call the witness at a later time.

"So noted." Judge Parker replied.

Clayton then called each marshal to the stand to testify as to the events that occurred on Mount Vista and to ask them how they had planned to respond to the threatened attack. One by one, J.H. Mershon, William P. Pittcock, Bud Kell and Heck Thomas, as well as Bass Reeves, all related the story about the shootout with the outlaws that left them all dead. Green Saunders and his wife Jane also testified to the truth of that event and the experience with Fred Cobb, who they identified in court.

John Marcum then cross-examined them. Then he began to cross-examine Bass Reeves. "Marshal Reeves, why were you looking for John Bruner and Frank Buck."

"I had warrants for them for horse thievery." Bass replied.

"Did they have big rewards out for them.?" Marcum asked.

"I think they were worth about $1,000 each." Bass answered.

"It is true you spend most of your time trying to kill men who have big rewards on them?" Marcum asked.

"That'd be true." Bass said.

"Have you ever killed anyone you were not supposed to kill?" Marcum asked.

Bass was a little unsettled by this question and showed it. "I killed my camp cook." Bass answered in a low voice. Members of the jury and the crowd, who may not have already heard about this, reacted with frowns.

"Objection, your honor!" Clayton stood up and shouted. "That matter has nothing to do with this trial!"

"What is the purpose of this line of questioning, Mr. Marcum?" Judge Parker asked. "And how is it relative to this case?"

"Your honor," Marcum replied, "it has to do with the credibility of the testimony given by the marshal in this trial. How can we decide against my clients based upon the testimony of a murdering marshal and a horse thief?"

"I would not get in the habit of calling one of my marshals a murderer, Mr. Marcum, if you plan to continue to practice law in this court! Is that understood, Mr. Marcum?" Judge Parker asked while staring coldly at the attorney.

"Yes, your honor, I understand." Replied Marcum. "I withdraw my question. I am done with this witness, but reserve the right to call him to the stand later." His ears were still stinging from the attack by Judge Parker, but he thought he'd made his point.

"The jury will disregard the last question asked of Marshal Reeves by Thomas Marcum, the attorney for the defendants." Judge Parker told the jury, while studying their faces for reaction. He knew the question had already damaged Reeves' testimony. Just because he told them to disregard the question did not mean they had forgotten it.

After all of the testimony was heard and the jury returned to the courtroom, it was time for the verdict.

"Foreman of the jury," Judge Parker said, "have you reached a verdict?"

"Yes, your honor." Replied the jury foreman.

"Please read the verdict to the court." Judge Parker ordered.

"Your honor," the foreman replied, "we, the jury, find the defendants *not guilty.*"

Judge Parker was not totally surprised. He knew that Marcum had done his job well. He had explored the weaknesses of the case and had managed to discredit some of the testimony. He did believe that the fear of punishment could be as powerful as the punishment itself. He believed that the trial would put Washington and McLish on notice that his court would not tolerate bad behavior without consequences.

The next day, an article appeared in the *Weekly Elevator* that said:

JUSTICE IS DONE!

As reported in this newspaper over 30 days ago, Billy Washington and Dick McLish, two hard working honest men, the prominent owners of the Washington-McLish ranch near Muskogee, were arrested by Deputy U.S. Marshal Bass Reeves and other marshals on a trumped up charge of attempted murder, without allowing them to establish their innocence and dragged around for days on the way to Fort Smith, with no foundation for a case against them. As stated before in this newspaper, Reeves treated them with disrespect and handcuffed them in front of their cowboys and other employees. We protested against all such proceedings by deputy marshals that are irresponsible towards our citizens.

Well, in a tremendous victory for justice, yesterday, Judge Parker's own jury trial, with testimony from those same marshals, has declared the defendants not guilty, just as we supposed in this newspaper some 30 days ago. We hope that Col.

Boles, the U.S. Marshal, will deal with these lying and murdering marshals in a firm way.

Once again, Judge Parker was furious when he read the paper the next morning. Maybe it was time to try Bass Reeves for killing his camp cook and get that behind them.

11

ANOTHER TRAIN ROBBERY

James Stuart was a white man who had just escaped from Texas lawmen and had managed to find an empty house where he and his woman could stay near Durant. He was forty-three years old and had made a living in the last 10 years stealing horses in Texas. He had killed one man for his money and had not yet been charged with that crime. James had managed to seduce a very nice looking 16-year-old girl who came along with him to Indian Territory in spite of everything her parents could do. Her parents were desperate to get someone to go look for her, but they were poor people without the means to hire a gunmen. All they could do was hope that she would eventually return to them safely.

Living nearby was the family of a negro freedman named Boyce Brown. He had married an Indian woman and they had two boys. One of them was a good boy who did anything he could to help his family. The other son was named Luther. Luther Brown was a very good sized boy, 6 feet tall and about 220 pounds. He was 17-years-old. His father had not been able to control him.

Luther was walking by the Stuart residence one day when he saw the 16-year-old white girl. He was struck by her beauty and decided he would drop by sometime to see if he could talk to her. The day he finally got up the courage to go up to the house, he was met at the door by James Stuart and he learned the girl had come from Texas with James. Over the next couple of weeks, Luther and James became friends and decided they would rob the Missouri, Kansas and Texas Rail Road, which stopped in Durant. They managed to find two other men who would rob the train with them.

The plan was for Stuart and Luther to ride to Muskogee and catch the train as it was headed south, back to Durant. Stuart would look around the train to see if there was any reason they could not rob it. If Stuart decided the train was okay to rob, he would go to the train engineer and put a gun to his head and make him stop just before the train got to Durant. The rest of the gang would be waiting there to help rob whatever there was to rob. Stuart and Luther rode to Muskogee after planning the attack and boarded the train as passengers. They would have a couple of days to check the train out and hopefully find out if there was any precious cargo on board. During the trip, Stuart learned that Fred Stone, a prominent Texas cattlemen, was aboard the train and was returning from Chicago, where he had managed to sell a herd of cattle that belonged to him. It was thought that he had close to $10 thousand in his saddlebags, which he had under his seat. His horse and the horses of the rest of his cowboys, were in a livestock car on the train.

To his dismay, Stuart also found out there was a Deputy U.S. Marshal on the train who had boarded at Muskogee. He was on his way to Texas to pick up a prisoner from the Texas authorities. The prisoner was a murderer who had left the Indian Territory to escape the marshal. Stuart was seated a few seats behind the marshal and decided that he would kill the marshal before he went to the front of the train to stop it. He did not think there were any railroad detectives or Pinkerton on the train. He figured the $10 thousand was worth the effort of robbing the train and was sure they could get some money from the rest of the passengers. He figured the cowboys also still had most of their pay from the cattle drive.

As the train got closer to Durant, James Stuart headed towards the front of the train. As he walked through the passenger car in which he was riding, he put his gun barrel to the back of the head of the U.S. Marshal and pulled the trigger. Blood and brain spattered the seat in front of the marshal and the bullet barely missed the woman in the seat in front of him. Immediately some of the cowboys jumped up with guns in their hands. When they did, he put a gun to their boss, Fred Stone's head, and told them to drop their guns, which they did. Luther was seated to the front of the car and had jumped up with his gun in his hand. Stuart told Luther to pick up the cowboy's guns and throw them out of the window, which he did.

Luther then covered everyone while Stuart went to the front of the train and put a gun to the head of the engineer of the train. The engineer did as he was told and stopped the train where he was told to stop it. Shortly, the other two members of the gang came riding up and helped rob the passengers. They found the $10 thousand where it was supposed to be, in Stone's saddle bags, and managed to get another $4 hundred from the passengers. After they were almost done with the robbery, a railroad detective who had been in the caboose came into the passenger car and managed to kill James Stuart. Luther killed the detective and he and the others rode away. The railroad didn't even put a reward on the outlaws. This was a small scale robbery as far as they were concerned, even though a railroad detective and a marshal were killed.

Judge Parker, on the other hand, was extremely upset as soon as he found out about what happened and issued warrants on the outlaws based upon their descriptions. The marshal who had been killed was Heck Thomas. Judge Parker wanted justice as soon as possible and decided to send Bud Kell and Bass Reeves to try to hunt the culprits down.

Luther was excited about the robbery. It was his first real crime and his share was almost $4 thousand. That was a lot of money. He also ended up with James Stuart's horse and decided to go back to Durant see if he could get Stuart's girlfriend to go with him. When he got to the house where Stuart was staying, the girl had ran outside when she had heard the two horses approaching. When she saw Luther leading an empty horse behind his she said,

"Where is James? Has he been hurt?"

"He was killed in the robbery." Luther told her.

"What am I going to do?" She screamed and started crying and shaking.

Luther comforted her and said, "I will take care of you. I have Stuart's share of the robbery money and I know he would have wanted me to take care of you."

"I want to go home to Texas!" She cried, sobbing madly, like she was about to explode with emotions.

"I will take you home." Luther said in a comforting tone.

"Will you really?" She cried.

"I really will." Luther responded in a kind voice.

Luther helped her put her meager belongings in a sack, which they tied to Stuart's horse and then helped the girl mount up. He was thinking about how he could get away from the law. Stuart had just escaped from Texas and someone was probably looking for the girl down there. He knew there was less law to worry about in the Indian Territory and he could probably move around more freely there. But he would attract a lot of attention riding around with a white woman with him. He should probably get rid of her, he thought. But not before having a good time with her.

After they had been riding for awhile, the girl asked him, "Are we headed to Texas? It seems like we are headed west, towards the sun."

"We are headed west right now," Luther told her, "but that is just to get the law off our trail. Once we get to a river, we will camp for the night and then head downstream in the water to cover our tracks."

When they got to the river, they made camp and tied the horses to a nearby tree. Luther had brought some makings for a stew and had managed to shoot a rabbit. After they had eaten, Luther put his arms around the girl and started kissing her on the neck. She tried to push him away, but he was much stronger than her. She screamed buy no one could hear her.

Once he had his way with her, she sobbed and trembled on the ground. He picked her up and carried her to the river and held her under the water until she drowned. He let her body go, floating towards Texas. It would be a while before she would be found, he thought.

The next morning, Luther headed towards Muskogee. He had some money in his pocket and his recent sexual encounter had whetted his appetite. He knew there were saloons in Muskogee where you could get any woman you wanted for $5. He could drink a lot of whiskey and have a lot of women with the money he had. After he tired of that, he could make a living selling whiskey to the Indians or stealing horses. He might even put together a gang and rob a train or two. He might even become famous.

Meanwhile, Bass Reeves and Bud Kell headed towards Durant. The last time Bass had been near Durant was when he was on the train that was robbed by Jesse James. He thought about that as they rode into town. They stopped first to visit with the Durant sheriff. The sheriff knew everyone in town and the surrounding area and was aware of the train robbery, since it had occurred nearby and some of the passengers from the train lived in Durant. He had questioned several of them after the robbery.

"Good morning, Sheriff." Bass said. "This is my fellow marshal, Bud Kell."

"Good morning Bass," The sheriff replied, "and good morning to you Marshal Kell."

The sheriff had met Bass before and had heard of Bud Kell, but it was the first time that they had met.

"What can I do for you boys?" The sheriff asked, even though he knew why they were there.

"Well," Bass began, "we are looking for three men who were with a Texas outlaw named James Stuart in a robbery of the rail road. Stuart killed Marshal Heck Thomas before he was killed by a railroad detective. A large negro man who was about my size killed the railroad detective, according to witnesses. We figure if we could find the large negro man, we could find the other two men. Do you have any idea who that large negro man could be?"

"I think that could be a young man named Luther Brown. He is the largest negro I have ever seen, besides you, Bass." the sheriff said, with a little chuckle.

"Not many men my size of any color." Bass acknowledged while chuckling a little bit himself. "Where do you think I could find this Luther Brown?"

"I can take you to his house." the sheriff volunteered.

"That would be great!" Bass responded.

The sheriff lead the way to the Brown home, with Bass and Bud following along. When they got to the Brown home, they were met at the front door by Boyce Brown.

"Good morning Sheriff," Brown greeted the men, "what can I do for ya'?"

"Boyce," the sheriff began, "these men are Deputy Marshal Bass Reeves and Deputy Marshal Bud Kell and they're here looking for Luther."

"What do they want with Luther?" Boyce asked.

"They think he was one of the men who robbed the Missouri, Kansas and Texas Rail Road train a few days ago. I am sure you've heard about that." he explained.

"Yep, I heard about that," Brown said, "but I don't know anything about whether Luther had anything to do with it. He did disappear about that time, and I haven't heard from him since."

"Do you know who he might have been travelling with?" Bass asked.

"He took a liking to a man from Texas who lived nearby." Brown responded. "He had a young woman living with him. I am not certain if they were married or not."

"Was the man's name James Stuart?" Bass asked.

"Yessir, that's the man's name!" Brown answered. "Was he in the train robbery?"

"He was killed in the train robbery." Bass responded.

"Luther may've been with him." Brown said. "We've had some problems with Luther. He was bad about getting into fights. And if he could get his hands on whiskey, he'd drink it until he was crazy. He is half Indian and drinking made him get real mean. We were afraid that man from Texas would help lead him in the wrong direction."

"Where did Stuart live?" Bass asked.

"He lived just down the road from here. "Brown said, "He'd moved into an abandoned house. It'd be the first house you come to. I guess the girl's still there."

"Thanks, Mr. Brown," the sheriff said. "We'll just mosey on down there."

When the men approached the house, they could see there were no horses there. They looked around and into the house and there was no evidence that anyone lived there anymore. They decided to go back to town and ask around to see whether anyone would know where the girl went or if they'd seen Luther.

When they got to town, they encountered some Chickasaw Indians who were looking for the sheriff. They started talking in Chickasaw, but the sheriff couldn't understand them. He looked at Bass and said "Do you speak Chickasaw?"

"Yes I do," Bass said, "they're talking about a white girl." Looking at the Indians, he asked them in Chickasaw, "What're you saying about a white girl?"

"We found the body of a dead white girl in the river," one of the men said. "We pulled her to the bank of the river, but it was clear she'd been dead for a while. We didn't know what to do with her, so we came to see the sheriff."

"Where's the body?" Bass asked.

"We'll take you to her." The Indian responded. "It'll be dark by the time we get there, unless we ride hard."

"We'll ride hard." Bass responded. "Sheriff, me and Bud will go with the Indians and bring the girl back. Maybe somone here will be able to identify her."

"Boyce Brown has seen her before." the sheriff responded. "I'll have him here by the time you get back tomorrow."

"Thanks." Bass replied. He and Bud followed the Indians, riding at a fast pace. Bass dreaded seeing the body as he thought of his own daughter. This would've been a good time to have a wagon along. Judge Parker granted them an exception to the rules and allowed them to leave with only two extra horses, instead of the normally required cook wagon and prison wagon. He wanted them to be able to cover as much territory as possible to find the men who had participated in killing his marshal. They wouldn't have been able to cover the distance required before dark with the wagons.

When they got to the river, they could see the girl's body still lying in shallow water. Luckily, no coyotes had found the body. The body was a horrible thing to see. Her skin was cold to the touch and was a powdery white color and some of the flesh had come off the bones. They decided to wrap her body in a blanket and the Indians fashioned a sled that could be dragged by one of the horses. As the sun started dropping below the horizon, they decided to camp for the night before heading back to Durant.

When they got back to Durant the following day and had arranged to have the girl's body taken care of, they let Boyce Brown look at her first. "That's the girl who was living with James Stuart," Brown said. "She came up here from Texas with Stuart. Her parents are probably looking for her. I know she couldn't be older than 16."

"It looks like her clothes were ripped apart. She was probably raped." Bass said.

"I hope it wasn't Luther that did this!" Boyce Brown said. "But that boy sure was staring at her, every time he saw her. He was talking about how good she looked." The old man started to cry.

The sheriff decided to send out a wire to Texas lawmen to see if the girl had been reported missing.

Bass asked the Indians, "Did anyone see a large negro man in the area where this girl was found?"

"Lighthorse saw a man like that heading towards the northeast from there." One of the Indians said.

"He's probably headed towards Eufaula or Muskogee." Bass said. Then he thanked the Indians for their help and gave them each a silver dollar.

"If I was an outlaw with money in my pockets," Bud said, "I'd probably head to Muskogee where there are women for rent and plenty of whiskey."

"That's probably where he's headed." Bass agreed. "We can ride up to Eufaula and check with the Lighthorse there. If he's there, or came through there, the Lighthorse will know where he is. They might not be able to retain him, but they'll follow him and keep track of him, if he doesn't belong there."

"Let's go get him." Bud said. He'd take pleasure in killing the man for what he did to the girl. Not to mention being a part of killing Heck Thomas. Bud hoped the man didn't give up too easy, so he could just shoot him. If he gave up, they'd have to go to trial and prove what he did. At least they had plenty of witnesses on the train. The outlaws were so stupid they didn't even wear masks. Of course they'd have been able to identify Luther just because of his size. It would be harder to prove what he did to the girl.

After talking to the Lighthorse in Eufaula, it was determined that Luther was headed for Muskogee. When they got to Muskogee, the Lighthorse told Bass that the man had been seen in a saloon. Walking into any saloon in Muskogee with a badge pinned on your chest was dangerous, to say the least. Not only would you be facing the man you were after, but you ran the risk that others in the saloon would like to see another marshal dead. When Bass and Bud walked into the saloon, Bass called out in his booming voice: "U.S. Marshals! Everyone keep your seat and stay away from your guns. We'll kill any man who draws on us." They spotted Luther sitting at a table with a woman on his lap. Without getting up, Luther drew his pistol and shot at Bass. Neither Bass or Bud wanted to take a chance of shooting the woman, so they ducked behind tables they turned up on their sides. Luther shot at them two more times before Bass thought he could shoot

Luther in the head without hitting the woman, who was kicking and screaming and trying to get away from him. BOOM! That was the last sound Luther ever heard.

The marshals dragged Luther out of the saloon without anyone else making a move towards their guns. Outside, they tied Luther to one of the extra horses and headed back towards Fort Smith; grateful they had emerged from the saloon alive. Other marshals had lost their lives there in the past.

Later, they found out the dead girl had been claimed by her parents and the other two men had been killed by someone who took their money and their horses. This case was closed...no trial to go to... no witnesses to locate. Just the way they liked it.

12

THE TRIAL OF BASS REEVES AND ROBERT'S MARRIAGE

"Bass," Judge Parker began, "I think it is time to get this matter of your camp cook out of the way. I think what we ought to do is to convene a Grand Jury to hear the testimony. If the Grand Jury fails to bring charges, then the matter will be deemed to be over. And the Grand Jury proceedings are closed to the public. What do think about that?"

"Judge," Bass responded, "I really don't think I have any say in the matter, but that sounds O.K. to me."

The Grand Jury was convened in October 1887. The prosecutor was M.H. Sandels and the defense attorney was Thomas Marcum. Marcum was with the law firm of Clayton, Cravens and Marcum. William H.H. Clayton had been the prosecutor in the Washington-McLish trial.

Again, it was time for Judge Parker to charge the jury, "Gentlemen of the jury, the laws of the United States can not be executed in this district until you as a Grand Jury first act in the premises. Before any action can be taken to ascertain finally the guilt of innocence of a man you must first accuse him in a lawful way by an indictment. That evidence is presented to you through the district attorney, or some one of his assistants and you pass upon the question primarily as to whether he shall be called upon in a court of justice to have the question determined as to whether he is guilty or innocent.

It is a principle of law, arising under the Constitution of the United States, that if man is the accused of a capital, or otherwise infamous offense, he can not be tried, no matter how guilty he may be, no matter how injurious to the community it may be not to try him, unless he is first indicted by a Grand Jury.

The Grand Jury system, in my judgement, is one of the finest guarantees of the citizen, in this country. At the same time it is a method by which it is made easier to determine the guilt or innocence of the party accused when he is put upon trial in a court before a Petit Jury.

The duties of this Grand Jury are much more onerous than those of a Federal Grand Jury. Here we have nearly all the Indian Territory attached to this jurisdiction. The criminals here committed some crime back at their homes and fled from justice, taking refuge in the land of the

Indians, where they have made a hot-bed of crime. The government, in its treaties with the Indians, obligated itself to keep all these characters out, or to remove them as fast as they moved in.

The U.S. Marshals serving this court have the task of cleansing this territory of these refugees. Now these marshals are not above the law more than any other, so therefore, we have before us Deputy U.S. Marshal Bass Reeves who has, by his own admission, killed his negro camp cook. It will be the task of this Grand Jury to indict him for that act, or not to indict him for that act, after hearing the evidence in the case as brought forward by testimony of the persons who happened to be at the scene of this act."

The first witness called by the prosecuting attorney, M.H. Sandels was the posse man, Bill Hayes.

"Mr. Hayes," Sandels began, "can you tell the Grand Jury what happened on the evening that William Leach was killed?"

"Well," Hayes began, "we'd camped for the night and me and the guard, Robert Brown, was in the process of getting all 11 of the prisoners out of the wagon and were handcuffing them to a long chain next to the prison wagon, where they could eat and sleep better, when I heard Bass and Leach arguing with each other about that little Indian dog that Bass kept with him most of the time. He liked to have that dog around so that it would bark and wake us up if anyone got near to us in the dark. We had a good fire going, and the cook had made some stew and some biscuits and Bass kept feeding that little dog pieces of biscuits. And then that little dog starts pestering the cook for a piece of stew meat he had laying on a board. Well, that cook threw a pan of hot grease on that dog and killed it and Bass jumps up and his rifle went off and it nearly shot the cook's neck off."

"Mr. Hayes," Sandels continued, "did Bass Reeves kill William Leach on purpose?"

"I don't know," Hayes answered, "whether he pulled the trigger on purpose or just jumped up and it went off. The hammer was cocked when he closed the chamber."

"Your honor, I am through with this witness." Sandels said.

"So noted." Judge Parker responded.

"Mr. Hayes," Thomas Marcum, the defender, asked, "do you think the entire incident with the camp cook could've been an accident?"

"Yessir." Hayes responded.

"Your honor, I am done with this witness." Marcum stated.

"So noted." Judge Parker replied.

"Mr. Brown," the prosecutor, Sandels asked, "can you tell us what happened on the evening that William Leach was killed?"

Robert Brown, the guard, recounted what he remembered from that night. "I'd just finished helping Bill Hayes get all of the prisoners out of the wagon, about 11 or so, I think, when the cook and Bass started arguing over a little dog that was begging for food from each of them. I thought it was the cook's dog, but someone told me later the little dog belonged to Marshal Reeves. Anyway, Marshal Reeves was working on his rifle, trying to dig a round out of the chamber, I think, and that camp cook threw hot greese on that dog and killed it. When that happened, the marshal jumped straight up in the air and his rifle went off, killing the cook. He didn't take aim like he normally does, he just jumped up and it looked like the gun went off by accident."

"Did Marshal Reeves pay you to say you thought it was an accident?" Sandels asked.

"No sir," Brown answered, "Marshal Reeves paid me and Bill $3 per day each to be possemen and guards and he never paid us anything else other than our normal pay."

"Your honor," Sandels said, "I am through with this witness."

"So noted." Judge Parker said. "Mr. Marcum, it is your turn to question the witness."

"Your honor," Thomas Marcum replied, "I have no questions for this witness."

"So noted." Judge Parker replied.

"Judge Parker," Sandels said, "may I approach the bench?"

"Both attorneys may approach the bench." Parker replied.

"Your honor," Sandels said, "these two men we just questioned are the only two credible witnesses in the case. I have talked to the 11 men who were locked to the chain outside the prison wagon and none of them are credible witnesses. Most of them didn't even look up until they heard the rifle go off. I don't have much choice except to rest this case, unless Bass Reeves will testify."

"Your honor," Thomas Marcum said, "Marshal Reeves does not have to testify against himself and I am inclined not to put him on the stand."

"Mr. Marcum," Judge Parker said, "I think Bass Reeves would like the opportunity to speak about this issue to the Grand Jury."

"Your honor," Marcum said, "I have advised my client not to testify and this court cannot compel him to testify against himself."

"So be it." Judge Parker said. "Then rest your case, Mr. Sandels."

"I rest my case." Sandels responded.

The jury was surprised they had such little evidence to hear. Several of them didn't like Bass Reeves, because they thought he was arrogant for a negro and thought they should convict him of something in spite of the lack of evidence. Most of them just wanted to go home. In the end, the only verdict they could come up with was "no indictment."

Bass was relieved. The judge was pleased.

"Well," Judge Parker said to Bass, "I am glad we have this behind us."

"Me too," Bass said, "I just want to go home." It would be dark in an hour, so he was in a hurry to get on the trail to Mount Vista.

Billy Washington and Dick McLish were having drinks in the saloon, with Bart Simms, the editor, when the first juror came back from the hearing.

"What happened?" Billy asked the juror.

"We didn't indict him," The juror responded.

"Why not?" Billy demanded.

"There just wasn't enough evidence to prove that he shot the cook on purpose!" The juror said, defensively.

"Where are the other jurors?" Billy asked.

"I guess they just went home," The juror responded.

"Would you give me an interview about what all happened at the Grand Jury hearing?" Simms asked.

"Sure," The juror responded.

The next day, the following article appeared in the *Weekly Elevator*:

A TRAVESTY OF JUSTICE

Yesterday, in what could only be called a farce of a Grand Jury hearing found Deputy U.S. Marshal Bass Reeves not guilty of murdering his camp cook, William Leach. One of the jurors, spoke to this reporter, with the understanding that his identity would not be revealed. He told this reporter that the government called only two witnesses, both of whom were in the employ of Bass Reeves, both of whom were paid by Bass Reeves, who swore the entire event was a tragic accident! There were 11 other witnesses to this event, who were not employed by Bass Reeves, who were not called as witnesses. The cowardly Bass Reeves himself refused to testify in his own defense! That of all things should have let the jurors know what had been done was on purpose! Now Marshal Reeves is free to go and terrify other honest citizens with his guns. Now he is even allowed to train his son to be a murdering marshal. This is a travesty of justice and we demand better from the law!

Judge Parker was so mad he could hardly contain himself when he read the paper the next morning. He wished someone else would buy that newspaper and fire Bart Simms.

The next morning, when Bass got up, he could smell the bacon and eggs that Jenny was fixing him for breakfast. She was very happy the Grand Jury hearing was over and they had chosen not to indict him. She had been worrying about the trial ever since Bass had told her about killing the camp cook. After he shaved and trimmed his mustache and got dressed, Bass walked into the kitchen; sat down at the table and waited for the food. He could smell bisquits cooking and the smell blended with the smell of the bacon and eggs. He loved being at home and getting good home cooked meals again.

"Bass," Jenny began, "are you going to be around all day?"

"Yes." Bass replied, wondering why she was asking. Was she tired of him already... He knew that wasn't the case. She'd probably favor him retiring and staying home all of the time.

"Well," Jenny said, "I invited everyone over to dinner tonight, including Susan Brady, who is Robert's girlfriend."

"I think Robert thinks she's more than a girlfriend." Bass replied.

"I think they may be getting married." Jenny said. She wasn't sure if Bass knew that already.

"That's what Robert told me." Bass said, confirming that he knew.

"Well," Jenny said, "I didn't think you'd met her and I haven't been around her very much so I just thought the whole family should spend some time with her."

"You want to make sure she's good enough for him?" Bass asked, laughing.

"You know me too well," Jenny said, "I just want to get to know her better and make sure Robert isn't making a mistake."

"Well," Bass said, "It's his mistake to make. I knew right from the first time I laid eyes on you at Fort Gibson, that I was going to make you my wife."

"If you hadn't asked me to marry you," Jenny said, laughing, "I was going to ask you."

"That's good to know." Bass said. "Robert said Susan has already been looking for a house. And she picked out a house with 100 acres that I'd already told Green Saunders to buy to add to our ranch. I was going to make the house into some stables, but I guess we can just deed them the house and keep the land."

"Green told me he bought that land yesterday." Jenny said. "We ought to go look at it sometime today."

"When's the last time you rode a horse?" Bass asked. He knew she rarely left the mountain, except to go to Fort Gibson to see her friends and family there. Even then, Green usually took her in a horse and buggy.

"It's been a while," she said, "but I assure you I can still ride one."

After breakfast, they saddled Silver and Ruby; Bass let Jenny ride Ruby. It'd be good to see if Ruby would behave for her. He didn't want to give the horse to Susan until he was sure it would behave but he knew Jennie could handle the horse. They stopped to get Green on the way because Bass and Jennie weren't sure exactly where the property was, even though Bass knew it touched one of their pastures. It took them about 20 minutes to get to the bottom of the hill and reach the property. Jenny went into the house, followed by Bass and Green.

"This isn't a bad house for them to start out with." Jenny said. "I'll help them to fix it up. I think they want to get married next week while you are still here, Bass."

"That soon?" Bass said. "We could deed them the house for a wedding gift and I'm going to give Ruby to Susan for a wedding present."

"Really?" Jenny responded. "I thought you were crazy about that horse!"

"I am," Bass said, "but I just can't stop people from laughing at me about that horse's name. I'm either going to have to give that horse away or kill the next man who laughs about it. But I'm going to reserve the right to breed Ruby. Can you imagine the kind of colts we could get by breeding Ruby and Silver?"

"That would be interesting." Green said, wondering what color they would be.

"I noticed old Silver giving Ruby the eye." Jenny said, laughing.

"Me too." Bass said in a more serious tone.

When they returned home, Jenny would start fixing dinner and Bass and Green could talk about business. Green told Bass that he had to pay $15 per acre for the

100 acres, because it had a livable house on it. "I didn't think we'd have to pay over $5 per acre for it!" Bass said.

"Well," Green said, "someone else was trying to buy it and they wanted to live in the house, so they ran the price up. If it didn't have a house on it, we probably could've gotten it for $5 per acre." Green was hoping Bass wasn't mad about him spending that much.

"I'm sure the land will be worth that sooner or later," Bass said, "and the fact that Susan loved the house makes it worth that much to me." Green was relieved to hear him say that. About that time, Robert came to the house with Susan.

"Marshal Reeves, this is Susan Brady." Robert said, introducing Bass to his fiancé.

Bass got up out of his rocking chair on the porch and took Susan's hand which was extended to him. "Pleasure to meet you Susan," Bass said in that booming voice of his. "I can see why Robert is very fond you."

"Thank you, Marshal Reeves!" Susan responded, blushing slightly. "It is nice to meet you."

"When we're at home, you can call me poppa," Bass said, looking at Robert and then at Susan, "and as soon as you're married, Susan can call me poppa too. Robert, you don't have to call me Marshal Reeves unless we are in public somewhere. Susan can call me poppa anywhere." They all laughed about that. Susan was a very pretty lady with a light chocolate complexion and brown eyes. Her eyes lit up with personality. Bass figured she would be a handful.

"Also, Susan," Bass said, "did you see that really good looking red thoroughbred tied to the rail out front?"

"Yessir," Susan said, "that's a mighty fine horse."

"Well," Bass said, "on the condition that you let me breed her to Silver later on, I plan to give you that horse for your wedding present."

"Oh, I can't wait until we get married, Robert!" Susan said, looking up at him.

"Me neither." Robert said.

"And Jennie and I are going to give you the house on that 100 acres we bought outside of Van Buren for a wedding present."

"Oh," Susan said, "I thought that'd been sold to someone else and I've been sick about it. I didn't know it was you who'd bought it. I heard it was Green Saunders."

"Green Saunders is my brother-in-law. You will meet him tonight," Bass said, "he bought the property for us to extend our pastures. We can give you the house and an acre. I'll probably want Robert to work part time for me to keep an eye on the horses and pasture land we have down there. Green is married to my sister Jane; you'll meet her tonight also. They live in that first house on the right you passed gettin' here. Green manages our ranch. Jane can sew anything and keeps me in suits."

Soon, Green and Jane arrived and Jane helped Jenny set places at the table for everyone.

Jenny had fixed turkey and dressing, which might've been unusual for October. She was so thankful that Bass hadn't been charged with killing his cook she considered this to be an early Thanksgiving. Besides, her oldest son was getting married soon and she was thankful that he'd found someone as nice as Susan.

Everyone bowed their head as Bass began the prayer, "Dear Lord, thank you for bringing us all together safely on this great evening, and please bless this food. Thank you for Jenny and her great cooking and thank you for Jane and Green who look after things while I'm out rounding up outlaws in the territory and thank you for Judge Parker, who is carrying out your justice and making this a safer place to live. Dear Lord, we also thank you for bringing Susan Brady into Robert's life and wish that you would bless them and their marriage and make it as happy as mine and Jenny's. And Dear Lord, please continue to bless the rest of our children and may you keep them all safe along with the rest of us. Amen!"

As soon as everyone got their plate filled, the conversation began again. "Susan," Jenny said, "we've made a bed for you at Jane and Green's house. We don't want you and Robert to have to ride home in the dark. I hope your parents aren't expecting you back home."

"No ma'm" Susan said, "they expected me to stay overnight up here. I'm really looking forward to sitting on the porch and looking up at all those stars from up here."

"They really don't look much closer up here," Jenny said, "they must be a long ways away!" Everybody laughed at that.

"What are you kids going to do for furniture?" Jenny asked.

"We'll just do without until we have the money to buy some," Susan said, "my parents said we could have the bed

I have at home to sleep on. The house already has a stove and fireplace to cook on."

"Robert just got paid $5,000 for his first trip as a deputy marshal," Bass said, "you can buy a lot of furniture for that."

"Really?" Susan said, winking at Bass. "Wow, Robert, you must be a really good provider! I think I'm marrying the right guy!"

"I doubt that every trip will be that good," Robert responded.

"Well," Jenny said, "at least I guess you have all the money you need for furniture. And a pretty good nest egg. I'd like to go with you when you pick out the furniture. I love to shop for things like that. They make some pretty good furniture in Fort Smith."

"That would be fun," Susan said, "I love to shop also. And I'd like to get to know you better. Maybe you can tell me something I don't know about Robert."

"I could probably tell you about all of his faults!" Jenny said, laughing.

"That's what I want to know!" Susan said, also laughing.

"Uh-oh," Bass said, "these women are ganging up on you Robert! You'd better watch out!" Everybody laughed at that thought.

The next week, Robert and Susan were married and moved into their new house. Susan and Jenny had done a good job of furnishing and decorating. Jane had sewn up some nice curtains for the windows. She'd also made them a matching tablecloth for the kitchen dining table. Jenny had insisted they get a table that could seat up to 8 people. "Me and Bass and Jane and Green expect to get invited down here for dinner at least once a month." Jenny said.

"That's not a problem," Susan had said, "you and Bass have been very kind to help us get a house and furniture. And I just love riding Ruby. I think she prefers a woman riding her."

"I imagine she was happy to trade Bass for you," Jenny said, "you weigh a lot less than he does!"

13

A Dastardly Crime

Billy Washington and Dick McLish were sitting with Bart Simms at the saloon in Fort Smith, when he told them that Bass Reeves' oldest son, Robert, had gotten married and had become a deputy marshal.

"Where does he live?" Billy wanted to know.

"Bass bought them a house on the outskirts of Van Buren." Bart said.

"So they don't live on top of the mountain?" Billy asked.

"No," Bart replied, "I heard that Robert and his new wife, Susan, had that house picked out to buy when they got married and that Bass had already bought it when he found out they liked it, so he gave the house to them."

"Lets take a ride over there." Billy said.

"Why do you want to see their house?" Bart asked.

"I'm just curious." Billy said. So the three of them got on their horses and rode over there. "What does this Susan do? Is she just a housewife?"

"No," Bart replied, "she teaches school in Van Buren."

"So I guess she'd be home on the weekends?" Billy said.

"Probably." Bart said.

"Nice house." Billy said as they rode by. "Its kind of away from town and neighbors, he said." Bart bgan to wonder why Billy would even care about that. But, Billy had a plan in mind.

When they got back to the Washington-McLish ranch, Billy looked at Dick and said, "You know what I'm thinking about Robert and Susan Reeves' house?"

McLish looked at Billy like he was crazy and said, "Why would I know what you're thinking? And why would you be thinking about Robert and Susan Reeves?"

"Because I'm going to kill them." Billy stated.

"What!" Mclish almost screamed. "Are you out of your damn mind?"

"No," Bill said, "I told you I was going to get even with Bass Reeves if it was the last thing I did on this earth! And I meant what I said. This is a chance to get even with him, because he won't have anyone guarding their house. I can take a couple of men and ride over there and kill 'em, before they even know what hit 'em." He had an evil smirk on his face that told McLish that Billy wasn't kidding. He really intended to kill them.

"Well," McLish said, "don't count on my tangling with Bass Reeves again in any way. I've learned my lesson. And if you keep on messing with Reeves, he's going to kill you.

He let the court do his dirty work that last time, but I bet he'll come after you himself if you harm his son or any of his family. You'd be better off trying to kill Bass himself."

"I can hurt him worse by killing his kid." Billy said. "Let him be the one to go to bed every night knowing he got his kid killed. Let him be the one to toss and turn every night thinking about it."

"I don't want to know anything about it," McLish said, "that way I don't have to lie about it in court, if it goes to a court. You will be lucky if he does put you on trial. I think this time, he'll take the law into his own hands."

"I don't think so," Billy said, "I think he'll hide behind his Judge and his marshals like he did the last time. This time, I'm going to go over there myself and make sure the job gets done. When I'm done, there'll be no witnesses to testify against me. Bass is too big of a coward to come after me by himself."

"I think you're wrong about that." McLish said. "You can't believe the stuff you read about him in Simm's newspaper. He's not a coward. He's like a rattlesnake who will be coiled up ready to strike you, if he finds out who killed Robert and Susan."

"We'll see who's right. And he won't find out who did it. We won't leave any witnesses." Billy said. "We still have a few people coming around from those posters in Muskogee. I'm gonna' find myself two mean sons-of-bitches to go with me. Now I know where they live and I know they should be there next weekend… That's when I'll do it… I'll wait until they've gone to bed and then we'll kill 'em.

We may have some fun with that Susan before we kill her… that'll be fun."

The following Saturday afternoon, Billy Washington rode into Fort Smith with two men from Texas who were wanted on murder charges. He'd paid them $500 each to help him. They were mean looking. They were such evil men that Billy didn't like them riding behind him. When they got behind him, it made the hair stand up on the back of his neck. Even Bass would be scared to death of these two, he thought. The three of them arrived in Fort Smith and went to the saloon to have a few drinks to make them even more mean. Billy knew it was a 5-mile ride to Van Buren, so they would leave Fort Smith about an hour before dark.

Billy couldn't wait to get to Robert Reeves' house. He could imagine the fear in Robert's face when he realized they were going to have their way with his wife before they killed him. The men planned to make Robert watch; that would make it even more exciting. Billy was almost drooling thinking about Susan. It'd been a long time since he had raped a woman and he missed the feeling of control and fear. After they were finished, they would choke her to death and let Robert hear her screams before they shot him.

After several whiskeys, the men headed for Van Buren. They stopped before they reached the Reeves property, dismounted their horses and tied them to a tree and walked to the house. There was just enough moonlight for them to see where they were going. As they got to the house, they found an open window and one by one stepped into the house as quietly as they could. The men could barely see where they were going once they got inside. All of the curtains were drawn, so very little moonlight filtered into the house. Billy had brought a candle and lit it. By the candle light, they determined they were in the kitchen. They looked around until they came to a closed door that probably was the bedroom. They slowly entered the bedroom, being careful not to touch anything. When Billy held the candle over the bed, he realized that Susan was alone.

Billy figured Robert must've gone somewhere and she was there by herself. It looked like they would at least have fun with her, before they killed her. He jerked back the covers and revealed her dark body, with no clothes on. Her eyes opened and she screamed as loud as she could. "It won't do you any good to scream, little girl." Billy said, with an evil laugh, "Nobody can hear you way out here!"

About that time, three shots rang out. Boom! Boom! Boom! The sound was deafening. The two men who were with Billy dropped to the floor dead and a bullet cut through Billy's ear. Robert had gone out back to check on the horses because he heard them tromping around like they were nervous. He thought maybe a coyote or a cougar was bothering them and had taken his gun belt. When he heard Susan scream, he'd bounded like a cat back into the house and into the bedroom. The candle had illuminated the men well enough that he was able to shoot two of them. Billy dropped the candle when the bullet hit his ear as he screamed like a girl. Some of the blood from the men splattered on Susan and the bed.

Billy jumped though the window of the bedroom and hit the ground running, like the true coward that he was. Robert fired two more shots at him as he ran down the road, but he couldn't see the sights on his pistols very well, so he missed. He was certain the man who escaped was Billy Washington. His face had been illuminated by the candle he was holding. It was a hard face to forget. He looked like pure evil. Robert figured he would track that bastard down in the morning and kill him. Right now, he was trying to console Susan. "Don't worry, honey, he isn't coming back. The two guys with him are stone cold dead. I'll drag them out back and worry about them in the morning. If the coyotes get 'em... who cares?"

"Oh my God!" Susan said, shaking and crying all at the same time. "Is this what its going to be like married to a marshal?"

"They won't dare come here again!" Robert declared. "Judge Parker said it's the fear of punishment that stops crime. Nobody will have the nerve to try this again. When Poppa hears about this, he'll probably go straight to the ranch and kill Billy Washington. Don't you worry about anything tonight. I'll be here with you." Their ears were still ringing from the gunshots. After changing the sheets and cleaning the blood off Susan, they went back to bed. They slept very little as Susan kept sobbing in fear.

Susan stuck to him like glue. Robert had to practically pry her off him the next morning when he got up. She got up as soon as he did and didn't want him to leave her. "I'll wait for you to get dressed, honey," Robert said, "and then I'll take you up to Poppa's house and see what he thinks we should do. You can stay there until you feel better about coming back home. You should probably stay up there any time I am out of town." She didn't argue with him. She would feel safer up there for the time being.

After Robert got dressed and went outside, he could see the horses the men had tied to a tree before slipping into the house. Billy had taken his horse and left. Robert retrieved their horses and brought them back to the house. He tied the men to the horses and tied the horses to the rail in front of the house. He decided to keep their gun belts to turn in, just in case they had rewards on them; Bass taught him that. If you have to kill someone, you may as well get paid for it.

Then Robert saddled up his horse and Susan's and they rode up to Mount Vista, with the two dead outlaws on their horses, trailing behind. When they got to the Indian guard at the bottom of the hill, he ran up to them, saying "What happened Mr. Robert?"

"We had some unwanted visitors last night and I killed 'em."

When they got to the second Indian guard at the top of the hill, he ran and asked the same thing. Then he went with them to Bass's house and ran up to the house banging on the door. "Mr. Bass! Mr. Bass! Come quick!" The Indian was much more excited than Robert. By this time he and Susan had settled down emotionally. Time had calmed their nerves.

Bass came outside, trailed quickly by Jenny. Both had worried looks on their faces. "What happened?" Bass asked, looking at each of the men to see if they were familiar.

"Billy Washington and these two men broke into our house last night. They went into the bedroom and had Susan pinned down on the bed. They must have thought I was gone, but I'd gone outside to check on the horses, because they were nervous and I thought a coyote or cougar was stalking them. Anyway, I took my guns with me and when I heard Susan scream, I ran back into the house and killed these two. Billy jumped out the bedroom window and ran off. I shot at him once in the house and twice after he jumped out the window, but he got away. He never returned my fire. I found some blood trailing him to his horse this morning, so I must've hit him."

"What time last night?" Bass asked.

"We'd just been in bed about 30 minutes," Robert replied. Jenny had helped Susan down from her horse and was hugging her. She was crying again, just thinking about what almost happened to her and remembering the men had seen her naked. "I decided to just wait until daylight to see what you thought we ought to do," Robert continued.

"You did the right thing." Bass said. "You couldn't have tracked him at night. His horse would take him back to his ranch in the dark. Your horse would want to go back home."

"What should we do now?" Robert asked.

"We're going to kill Billy Washington." Bass said.

"Shouldn't we get more marshals?" Robert asked.

"This is personal and this has to stop... right now. The only way to stop it is to kill Billy Washington. We've tried to stop this the right way, and it didn't work, so now it's time for us to take this matter into our own hands." Bass stated. "Are you with me Marshal Rob?"

"Let's go get 'em Marshal Reeves." Robert replied. "They'll probably have a lot of men."

"They only have about 5 or 6 gunmen who are killers," Bass said, "those cowboys won't interfere. We can handle 'em."

"I'm with you," Robert said.

"It'll take us a couple of days to get there and we may have to kill 6 or 8 men, so we probably ought to take a cook wagon and a prison wagon." Bass said, "We can leave this morning and go by Fort Smith and pick them up on the way. Is there anything you need to do at your house before we leave?"

"No sir," Robert answered.

"Jenny," Bass said, "take care of that girl until we get back!"

"Don't worry," Jenny said, "I will."

Robert kissed Susan and he and Bass mounted their horses and headed to Fort Smith.

After arriving in Fort Smith and arranging to have the dead men buried, Bass rounded up the cook and the cook wagon and got it loaded with supplies. They might be gone for awhile if they had to chase Billy Washington further than the ranch. Bass also located a posse man to drive the prison wagon and guard the camp.

It took them two days to reach the Washington-McLish ranch. When they arrived at the property line, Bass left the cook and cook wagon and the posse man and the prison wagon a short distance from the line, near some trees. As long as the cowboys didn't cross the property line, they wouldn't be able to see the wagons.

14

The Shootout

Billy Washington had ridden his horse straight to the ranch without stopping. He'd finally stopped his ear from bleeding by tying a bandana around it, but he had blood all over his shirt when he came riding up to the ranch.

"Damn!" McLish said when he saw Billy come riding up and dismount, "What happened to you? Are you hit bad, do you need a doctor?"

"We got into the house," Billy said, "but that son-of-a-bitch kid somehow was waiting on us and killed the two men with me. He shot me in the ear!"

"It looks like you'll survive." McLish said. "I told you it was stupid for you to go over there and mess with the Reeves! Now I bet Bass Reeves is headed this way to kill you."

"What do you think we should do?" Billy asked.

"What do you mean what should we do? There is no *we*. I'm not involved. And it's too damn late for you to be thinking about what to do now!" McLish said. "You should've listened to me. I'm fixing to get on a horse and ride to Muskogee and stay in a hotel until this is all over. I don't want anything to do with an angry Bass Reeves. You've stirred up a hornet's nest and you're going to get stung. In fact, you already got stung. Now you're going to get killed!" McLish wasn't going to risk his life because of something stupid that Billy did.

"We still have 5 killers that work for us." Billy said. "I think we can hold them off. I'll offer them a $5,000 reward if they kill him."

"You've already wasted too much money trying to get even with Bass Reeves!" McLish said. "I'm not paying for any of this. If you want to waste your money on Bass Reeves that's fine. You probably won't live to pay them anyway." McLish then got his horse saddled and headed to Muskogee.

Billy Washington thought about just getting on a horse and going to Muskogee himself, but he was determined to kill Bass Reeves no matter what. He went into the bunkhouse where the gunmen were staying and told them what was about to happen.

"Bass Reeves will probably be here tomorrow sometime." Billy said, "I'll pay each of you $500 to stay and help me kill him. I'll pay a $1,000 to each of you once Bass Reeves is dead. If you don't stay and help me, you'll no longer have a job. Who's gonna' stay and who's with me?"

All of the killers thought the odds were good and decided to stay. "So what's your plan?" One of them asked.

"Well," Billy began, "Bass is really good with a rifle, so if we stay inside the buildings and try to hold him off with rifles, he would be able to pick us off one by one from a distance. But if 5 of us go outside and let him get close enough to draw pistols, we should have an advantage because there will be 5 of us against him or him and his son. At close range, we should have the advantage. We'll put one man with a rifle in the hay loft. When they get into pistol range, the man in the loft can take out Bass with a rifle. Then our odds will be even better." The men agreed to the plan. The best man with a rifle was selected to be in the loft. They told their cowboys to keep an eye out for Bass and to send somebody on the run to let them know when he got to the property line.

The next day, just before noon, a cowboy came riding up to the ranch letting Billy know that Bass Reeves was on the way. The 4 gunmen and Billy sat on the front porch of the ranch house to wait on them.

"Marshal Rob," Bass began, "when we ride up to the ranch we have to be prepared for anything. There's not much cover we can get behind. They could stay inside and shoot with rifles from a distance, or they might stay outside to see what we're going to do. There'll probably be 6 or 7 of 'em. Our only cover is some water troughs about 50 yards from the house.

What we'll do, is to ride up as close as we can without somebody shooting. Most men can't hit you with a rifle riding on a horse much more than 100 yards with iron sights. If they start shooting when we're that far out, we'll hit the ground and lay flat. That way, we'll be harder to hit. Our horses might run off, but we'll just have to deal with that when the time comes. With a rifle, I think we can pick them off one by one from 100 yards out.

Billy may just give himself up and let us arrest him, but that's not likely. If I were him, I would face us at a close distance because that would give them an edge, having more gunmen. I'd be surprised if they didn't hide one or two men somewhere with a rifle to pick us off as we ride closer. That's what I'd do.

We'll just have to keep our eyes open and try to spot anyone they may have hidden. If we see a rifle move somewhere or anyone goes for their pistol, we need to start shooting as fast as we can. I trained you to shoot well and I think we can take 'em without getting ourselves killed. If we don't do this, we'll be forever having to worry about these men sneaking up on us somewhere else. It needs to end here. Good luck son."

"Good luck to you, Marshal Reeves... Poppa."

When they were within 200 yards from the house, they could see men on the front porch. "It looks like they're going to do what I thought they would." Bass said. "Keep your eyes open for any movement from any windows."

"Yes sir." Robert replied. He was nervous, but was confident they could handle the situation.

As they rode to about 40 yards of the ranch house, Bass saw movement in the hay loft of the barn. In a flash, he drew his Colt .45s and killed the man in the loft. As Bass went for his Colts, everyone began to draw. At the same time that he killed the man in the loft, he killed the first man to clear his holster with his other pistol. Billy Washington and the other 3 men were drawing their pistols, when Robert killed Billy with his first shot, hitting him right between the eyes with the pistol in his left hand; shooting another man in the chest with his second shot from the pistol in his right hand. One of the men managed to shoot Robert's horse as it reared up and one of the men managed to shoot Bass in the arm. Bass killed one of those men with his third shot from the pistol in his left hand and then the last one with the pistol in his right hand. As Bass tied a bandana around his arm to stop the flow of the blood, Robert struggled to get out from under his horse. The horse had fallen on his leg and had him pinned against the ground. Bass got off his horse to make sure Robert hadn't been shot.

"Have you been shot son?" He asked. His ears were still ringing from all of the gunfire and the burned gunpowder filled the air with small clouds of smoke.

"I don't think so." Robert responded. "But I can't feel my leg. I can't get my leg out from under the horse." Bass continued to scan the house and other buildings to make sure there weren't any more men.

"Just stay calm," Bass said, "I think I can tie a rope to your saddle horn and get Silver to pull your horse up enough to get you free. After a few attempts, Bass was finally able to get Robert free of his horse. There was no blood, so they figured he was O.K. except for some serious bruising. "I had a horse roll over on my leg one time," Bass said, "and it swelled up like a rattlesnake had bit me. That's going to hurt a lot, but you should be alright."

"Right now, it's just numb," Robert said, "it doesn't hurt at all."

"It will!" Bass said. "I'll go back and get the wagons. I don't see any more guns sticking out of windows, but you should keep your guns handy just in case. I'll help you up on the porch, where you can sit with your back to some wood."

After fetching the wagons, Bass and the posse man loaded the 6 dead men into the prison wagon. Bass searched the house and all of the buildings, but there were no others. Billy Washington was among the dead men, but Bass hadn't seen Dick McLish. He guessed Dick didn't want anything to do with what happened. He'd probably left until this was over.

When they got back to Fort Smith, Bass went in to see Marshal Boles and explained what happened.

"You know Judge Parker isn't going to be happy about this," Boles said.

"I know that," Bass answered. "I had enough of Billy Washington trying to harm me or my family every time he got the chance; I got to where I couldn't sleep at night."

"I don't blame you for doing it." Boles said. "It's probably what I would've done. I don't expect for there to be any charges filed against you. But Judge Parker isn't going to like it. And I'm sure that crazy newspaper editor, Bart Simms, is going to have a good time writing about it."

"I haven't lost any sleep from any of those articles he wrote," Bass said. "but I'm worried about what Judge Parker might do."

"You better go see him," Boles said.

"I hear you've brought in a whole wagon full of dead men," Judge Parker said. "And I see that you got yourself shot in the arm."

"Yessir." Bass said.

"Was Robert hurt?" Parker asked.

"His horse was shot and it fell on his leg," Bass said, "but there are no broken bones, so he'll be O.K. after some time off."

"Well," Judge Parker said, "you're both going to get some time off. I'm taking your badges. We simply can't have vigilante law in the territory. Do you understand that?"

"Yessir." Bass responded. "Will there be any charges filed?"

"If Dick McLish wishes to file charges, we'd probably convene a Grand Jury to see if they had enough evidence to indict you. There are no witnesses who are alive, other than you and Robert. And if you two were charged, you wouldn't have to testify. My guess is that McLish will be happy to own the ranch by himself and this'll be the end of all this nonsense. When you leave here, leave your badge and bring me Robert's badge before you leave town." The judge hated to do this, but thought that he must.

"Yessir." Bass said. He was depressed by the conversation but had expected to lose his badge. He'd hoped Robert would get to continue to be a marshal, but he wasn't going to argue with the judge. When he took Robert's badge from him, he thought he saw tears well up in his eyes. He wasn't very far from shedding a tear when he handed Robert's badge to Judge Parker.

"Don't worry," Bass said after that, talking to Robert, "we can make a living on the ranch. I've been preparing for my retirement and there's enough for all of us to live on."

"Thanks, poppa." Robert said. "But I sure will miss going out after the outlaws with you."

"We can spend our time looking for good horses." Bass said, smiling at Robert. "Besides, I miss you calling me poppa."

Meanwhile, Bart Simms sat down to write about the incident for the next day's *Weekly Elevator*. The whole town was buzzing about what happened. He was worried that Bass might find out that it was he who told Billy about Robert's house and actually took Billy to the scene of the crime. If Bass found out that he'd taken Billy there, he'd probably be next on his list to come after. He decided it was time to make amends. The next day, the *Weekly Elevator* carried the following story:

Vendetta Results in Death of Billy Washington

"This newspaper has in the past been supportive of Billy Washington as a prominent citizen and rancher and has always held him in the highest respect. However, a recent event has caused this editor to change his opinion and to admit that he was badly wrong about Mr. Washington, and just as badly wrong about Marshal Bass Reeves. This newspaper had taken the stand that Marshal Reeves had wrongly arrested Washington on trumped up charges that he tried to

kill Marshal Reeves and that he also tried to kill the family of Bass Reeves.

All of that has changed with the news of recent events. It seems that Billy Washington and two of his hired killers attempted to rape marshal Robert Reeves' wife and perhaps kill her and her husband. Washington and his killers were caught red-handed while trying to rape Susan Reeves. She was screaming at the top of her lungs, just like any prudent woman would when confronted with such dastardly actions. Fortunately for her, Robert Reeves had stepped outside to check on the horses which were acting up as if wild animals were after them. Hearing Susan scream, Marshal Robert Reeves bounded back into the house and then killed two of the men and wounded the other, who Robert identified as Billy Washington. He was able to identify Washington by the light of a candle.

Two mornings later, still in hot pursuit of this villainous scoundrel, Bass Reeves and Robert Reeves were confronted by Billy Washington and 6 killers trying to take their lives. The Reeves then shot and killed all of the men trying to kill them. This newspaper applauds such courageous action by these brave men. We have been wrong in the past and we admit it. There is no worse crime, even murder, than taking an innocent woman by force. It is barbaric and should be condemned by all.

Meanwhile, Judge Isaac Parker has stripped these men of their badges because they pursued the men without warrants from the judge. It is the position of this paper and many citizens of Fort Smith that the marshal's badges were wrongly taken, since they needed no warrants because they were in hot pursuit from a witnessed crime and urge Judge Parker to change his position and give these two brave men back their badges. Every man in this territory is urged to take this position with Judge Parker and urge this action."

Judge Parker was mildly amused by the article in the *Weekly Elevator*. That guy is an idiot, Parker thought to himself. To be so highly educated and surrounded by so many stupid and uneducated people was almost a curse to the judge. He sometimes lost his patience with people as a result of that. He had to really hold back his temper. It was his job to maintain stability and he must set a good example. So now Bart Simms is Bass Reeve's biggest supporter?. That was downright funny to some degree. Simms still doesn't like me, Parker thought. But that's O.K. Maybe Simms had actually done the judge a big favor. He hated to take Bass and Robert's badges, since they were now two of his finest marshals. Maybe the article by Simms would turn the public sentiment towards giving them back their badges. He was certainly willing to consider that.

Judge Parker was simply not prepared for the outpouring of support for giving Bass Reeves and his son their jobs back. Standing before him, in his office, were the heads of the Cherokee Nation, the Choctaw Nation, the Creek Nation, the Osage, the Chickasaw, the Commanche, Kiowa and Apache as well as the Cheyenne and Arapaho tribes, in full battle dress. Through an interpreter, they all conveyed their strong desire to have Bass Reeves reinstated as a marshal.

"Marshal Reeves, big friend of Indians," was the common message. All of these chiefs, had caused quite a stir in Fort Smith, when they passed through town on their way to the courthouse.

Judge Parker had to stop himself from crying. Despite all of his efforts, he had tears in his eyes he couldn't control.

"Judge Parker, also big friend of Indians. Not mad at Judge Parker, just want Bass Reeves back," the chiefs stated.

Judge Parker had spent his recent life trying to clean up the Indian Territory where those poor maligned Indians could live in peace. It was the first time that the Indian Nation had expressed their personal appreciation for what he was trying to do. He felt warm all over due to the thanks they were giving him. He knew they were sincere.

Speaking through the interpreter, Judge Parker replied to their request, "It is for the sake of the Indian Nation that this court exists. It is our purpose to cleanse the Indian Nation of bad people, whether they be black, white or Indian. We are working for your benefit. Because of that, it would be impossible for me to ignore your request. In fact, I cannot ignore your request and I hereby promise the chiefs of all these Indian Nations that I will grant your request. If Marshal Reeves and his son will accept their badges back, then this court will reinstate them. This court is honored by your presence and offers a sincere invitation to return at any time and express any opinions you may have regarding this courts behavior in its task."

All of the Indian chiefs smiled and did something resembling a war dance. But Parker knew that it was a dance of joy. He was tempted to join them in their celebration, but thought better of it. He was overjoyed himself. This was the excuse that he needed to reverse his position and reinstate Bass and Robert. He couldn't wait to see those badges pinned on those men again. He immediately dispatched Marshal Boles to the Reeves ranch to convey the offer. He truly hoped they would accept. He knew that Bass was planning to retire soon, but having his son to train might get him to stay longer. He hoped so.

At the Reeves ranch, the mood was somber as they discussed what had happened over the past days. The whole family, including Robert and Susan, was sitting down for dinner as Marshal Boles rode up. "Do you have enough food for another hungry soul?" Boles asked as he walked in the door.

"You know you're always welcome in this house and at this table," Jenny said. "There isn't a person in this house who doesn't look up to you and respect you," Jenny continued, "no matter what's happened. We understand what you and Judge Parker had to do," she said, "and we don't hold any bad feelings. In fact, you can tell Judge Parker that I've been waiting to fix a big pecan pie, because we needed some extra help to eat it. Bass would rather have my fried peach pies," she said, winking at Bass.

"That's true," Bass said, "about the fried pies, and about there being no hard feelings about what happened."

"Well," Boles said, "you aren't going to believe what happened today."

"What happened today?" Bass asked. Everyone turned to look at Boles.

"The chiefs from every Indian Nation rode to Fort Smith today, in full battle dress." Boles related.

"Oh my God," Jenny said, "what has happened to cause that? Are the Indians uprising?" She had grave concerns, since the Creek were her people.

"Yes they are!" Boles declared, with a serious look on his face. "They're ready to go to war to get Bass reinstated as a Deputy U.S. Marshal!"

"What?" Jenny exclaimed, "what do you mean by that?"

"Well," Boles said, suddenly smiling, "the chiefs all came to Fort Smith to see Judge Parker and demand that he give your badges back," he said, looking at Bass and then at Robert. "I brought them to you…will you take them back?" Boles could see that Bass had reservations about taking the badge back and he could see that Bass was looking at Robert to see his reaction.

"Marshal Reeves," Robert said, "it'd be my pleasure to serve under you again."

That did it. "Marshal Rob," Bass said, "it'd be my pleasure to work with you as a marshal again. I'll stand side by side with you in battle with pride." He gave a big smile to everyone in the room. He could see that Jenny and Susan were not as happy about this as he and Robert. But, they'd be okay with it. They knew their men were happier when they were chasing outlaws.

Marshal Boles then walked around the dinner table and pinned a badge on Bass and then on Robert. Then everyone cheered and clapped their hands and Bass said,"Jenny pass me one of those fabulous fried pies of yours!" For the first time of the night, Jenny had a big smile on her face.

After dinner, Colonel Boles told the family that he had a gift for them. They followed him out of the house to where his horse was tied. Tied on each side of the saddle were sacks that turned out to have two small puppies in them.

"These are American Pit Bull Terriers," he told them, "The American Pit Bull Terrier is a mix between terriers and bulldogs. These dogs were bred in England and arrived in the United States with the founders. We used them in the Civil War to help guard us at night. They'll wake you up if anyone or anything approaches you in the dark." The dogs were pure white, just like Silver, and wanted to lick everyone who picked them up.

"Just what we needed!" Bass said. "I've missed my little dog."

The End